HELPING FOSTER CARERS TO MANAGE CHALLENGING BEHAVIOUR

Evaluation of a cognitive-behavioural training programme for foster carers

Part of the

Institute of Health

and Social Care Research

Peninsula Medical School

University of Exeter

CEBSS

Centre for Evidence-Based Social Services

by

Geraldine Macdonald
Ioannis Kakavelakis
University of Bristol

Prepared for
**The Centre for Evidence-Based Social Services,
Peninsula Medical School, University of Exeter,
2004**

Address for Correspondence

Professor Geraldine Macdonald
Director: Information and Knowledge Management
Commission for Social Care Inspection
33 Greycoat Street
London
SW1P 2QF

Tel: 0207 979 2117 (London)
Tel: 0113 220 4672 (Leeds)

E-mail: Geraldine.Macdonald@csci.gsi.gov.uk

About the authors

Geraldine Macdonald is Director of Information and Knowledge Management at the Commission for Social Care Inspection, and Visiting Professor both of the Centre for Evidence-Based Social Services and the University of Bristol. She was Professor of Social Work at Bristol for the duration of this research project. Her research interests include the evaluation of the effects of social interventions, particularly social work, decision-making in child protection and ethical issues in social work research and practice.

Ioannis Kakavelakis is a researcher at the School for Policy Studies, University of Bristol, and a Counselling Psychologist. He has a background in social psychology. Both his Ph.D. and post-doctorate work focused on the examination of cognitive mechanisms operating in social influence contexts. His research interests include the evaluation of psychotherapeutic approaches and systematic reviews in health care and social policy.

To obtain further copies of this report, please contact:

Centre for Evidence-Based Social Services
University of Exeter
Peninsula Medical School
Haighton Building
St Lukes Campus
Exeter
EX1 2LU

Tel: 01392 262865
E-mail: Sue.Bosley@pms.ac.uk

ISBN 0-9535709-7-5

£6.99

Contents

List of figures and tables

Acknowledgements

This project is the product of some visionary directors of social services in the South West of England, concerned to improve the quality of services and of decision making in the departments for which they are responsible, and willing to take the risk of an undertaking which many doubted was feasible. The sceptics have been proved wrong. The realisation of this experimental study of the effectiveness of cognitive-behavioural training for foster carers has rested on the shoulders of many people. We are particularly grateful to the foster carers who participated in this study. We learned a great deal from the carers who participated in the training, and we thank them for their hard work. Especial thanks are due, however, to those in the control group. These carers met with the researcher on three separate occasions, completed questionnaires, patiently answered questions and shared their views even though there was no immediate benefit in terms of training – which they very much wanted. It is altruism of this kind that underpins the most rigorous of evaluations, and we thank them for their generosity.

Tribute should also be paid to the staff in each of the departments who smoothed the path for us, and helped us overcome a number of difficulties. Members of the Steering Committee for the Project were generous with their time and we are sorry that towards the end of the project time pressures limited their input into this report. We are happy to make amendments in the light of their wise comments and observations.

Finally, thanks are due to Professor Martin Herbert both for agreeing to lead the training and for allowing us to draw both on his wealth of clinical experience and his previous work, including material that formed the basis of the training programme and supporting handbook.

Executive Summary

---

1. Introduction (Chapter1)

1.1 Children looked after have consistently fared less well than others on a range of indicators, including health, education, and social adjustment. One of the factors which increases children's risk of adverse outcomes is lack of placement stability. Unplanned terminations of placements and frequent changes of carers can undermine children's capacity to develop meaningful attachments, disrupt friendships, and contribute to discontinuities in education and health.

1.2 Children looked after have long been recognised as experiencing high rates of behavioural and emotional problems. Among the many reasons why behaviour problems matter is that they are strongly correlated with unplanned placement endings.

1.3 Previous research has also highlighted the need for foster carers to be better equipped to manage the range of demands placed on them by children with emotional and behavioural problems.

1.4 This study was designed to test whether training foster carers in methods designed to help them manage challenging behaviour would be helpful to them and beneficial for looked-after children. Whilst primarily concerned to test whether it enabled carers better to manage difficult behaviour, we were also interested in whether it would enhance carers' confidence in their capacity to care for challenging children and young people and, ultimately, whether improved skills and/or confidence would enhance placement stability.

2. Managing Challenging Behaviour (Chapter 2)

1.1 Cognitive-behavioural training was chosen on the basis of its track record of effectiveness in dealing with a wide range of emotional and behavioural programmes; its effectiveness in training birth parents (i.e. 'parent training'), and evidence from some previous studies of training foster carers

1.2   Typically, a cognitive-behavioural approach aims to help participants to develop i) an understanding of the ways in which behaviour can be shaped by the environment, ii) skills in analysing behaviour – commonly referred to as the ABC of behaviour[i], iii) selecting strategies to change the relationship between behaviour and its consequences and/or changing the antecedents (e.g. asking a child to get ready for bed after making it clear what his/her bedtime is and turning the television off before asking), and iv) monitoring and reviewing progress.

1.3   The study tested six hypotheses. These were as follows:

(i)   Participants in the training programme condition would score significantly higher on the Knowledge of Behavioural Principles as Applied to Children (KBPAC) scale than foster carers in the wait-list control condition.

(ii)   Participants in the training programme would be significantly more likely than foster carers in the wait-list control group to use behavioural techniques in managing children's behaviour.

(iii)   For children in the experimental group[ii] there would be fewer unplanned terminations of placement in which behaviour problems were implicated.

(iv)   Participants in the training programme would report a significant reduction in the range of problems that they found particularly difficult or challenging, compared with foster carers in the wait-list control.

(v)   Foster carers in the training programme would report success in dealing with behaviour problems.

(vi)   Foster carers would feel more confident in their abilities to manage difficult behaviour.

3. The Training Programme (Chapter 3)

1.1   The content of the training programme developed for this study mirrored that of programmes that have proved effective when provided to groups of parents facing difficulties with their children. More specifically it was based on an established programme developed by Herbert and Wookey (In press) for use with birth parents.

[i] Where 'A' represents 'antecedents, 'B' represents 'behaviour' and 'C' represents 'consequences.

[ii] The 'training group'.

1.2   The training sought to familiarise carers with social learning theory, both in terms of understanding how behaviour develops and how it can be influenced using interventions derived from social learning theory. There was an emphasis throughout on developing the skills to observe, describe and analyse behaviour in behavioural terms – the so-called 'ABC' analysis.

1.3   The programme gave due consideration to the fostering context, and to the particular constraints and pressures under which carers operate.

1.4   The programme was designed to promote a sense of confidence or 'self-efficacy'. Self-efficacy has been shown to be correlated with effectiveness.

1.5   The programme was originally designed as five weekly, three-hour sessions plus a follow-up session and this format was used for the first two groups. Because these groups felt rather pressured, we decided to move to four weekly, five-hour sessions plus a follow up for the remaining four groups. The content of the programme remained unchanged.

1.6   Each participant foster carer was provided with a Course Handbook. This contained details of each of the sessions and information relevant to each. It was written and presented in what we hoped would be an easily accessible format. Participants were asked to read certain sections between sessions as part of their 'homework', and had an opportunity to discuss the material at the beginning of each session.

1.7   The training was organised to reflect a collaborative approach to problem-solving, such as that described by Herbert and Webster-Stratton (Webster-Stratton 1998; Herbert and Webster Stratton 1994). The training was designed to marry the expertise and experience of foster carers with the specialist knowledge of the trainers and their experience of tackling child behaviour problems.

1.8   Two trainers ran the training programme: The lead trainer was a clinical psychologist who was experienced in working with troubled and troublesome children and young people. The other was a professor of social work who had a special interest in behaviour problems and looked after children.

1.9   The trainer supporting the lead trainer was the grant holder. To minimise bias, all data were collected and analysed independently by a researcher recruited specifically to the project.

4. Methodology (Chapter 4)

4.1 The most secure way of answering questions about the effectiveness of a particular intervention is by means of an experimental research design. The most common design is a randomised controlled trial, in which research participants are randomly allocated either to receive the intervention or to a group that does not. The latter is referred to as a control group.

4.2 This was the design used in this study. Carers who agreed to participate in the study were randomly assigned either to the training group (the experimental group) or a 'wait-list' control. Those in the control group continued to receive standard services and were told that should the training prove helpful, it would be made available to them in the future. The funders of the research – Directors of the South West Consortium – gave this undertaking.

4.3 The participants in this study were foster carers in six local authorities in the South West of England.

4.4 Although we initially received statements of interest from a large number of carers, this number dwindled for a variety of reasons. In addition to those who did not meet our inclusion criteria, some withdrew from the study once the dates and/or location of the training were confirmed. Others withdrew when told they had been allocated to the control group.

4.5 Final numbers of willing participants allowed us randomly to allocate them to the two conditions, but we had to do so on a 1 in 2 basis (rather than the 1 in 4 that we had intended), and we had to do so within geographical regions. This effectively means that we ran three small trials, rather than one.

4.6 The outcome measures used were:

(i) A measure of participants' knowledge of behavioural principles as applied to children (O'Dell et al. 1979). Details of this instrument can be found in Appendix 1.

(ii) The number of unplanned breakdown of placements. These data were obtained from interview data, which covered the month prior the onset of training, the five weeks of training, and the six months after training.

(iii) The Child Behavioural Checklist (Achenbach 1993).

(iv)   A Foster Carer Satisfaction Questionnaire.

7.7   Participants were interviewed before and after training, and at six months follow-up. Each interview schedule was developed specifically for the purpose of the study. All interviews were tape-recorded after consent was obtained.

5. Results (Chapter 5)   1.1   A preliminary analysis indicated no significant effects and/or interaction of the Local Authority variable with any other variables. Since no significant effect of this variable was observed, this factor was excluded from subsequent analyses.

1.2   117 participants comprised the final sample, of whom all but two were white. Of these, 67 foster carers participated in the training group (female foster carers = 52, male foster carers = 6, couple foster carers = 9) and 50 in the control group (female foster carers = 37, male foster carers = 6, couple foster carers = 7). The ages of these participants ranged from 32 to 65 years, with a mean age of 45 years. Experience of fostering (in years) ranged from one to fifty years, with a mode of one year (i.e. carers with one year's experience occurred more frequently than carers with other profiles). The overall mean was 8.68 years.

1.3   Two of the six hypotheses were clearly confirmed. These were hypotheses (1) that participants in the training programme condition will score significantly higher on the Knowledge of Behavioural Principles as Applied to Children Scale (KBPAC), and (6) enhanced confidence in their abilities to manage difficult behaviour.   The qualitative data collected from participants in the training group is the source of evidence for this last hypothesis.   Carers generally said that the course had made them more confident to deal with difficult situations and difficult behaviour.

1.4   The hypotheses concerning the use of behavioural techniques (Hypothesis 2) received support in relation to the use of ABC analysis, tokens and 'grounding'. Those who had participated in training were significantly more likely to be using ABC analyses at all time points measured (i.e. post-test and follow-up) compared with those in the control group. They were also more likely to use tokens and less likely to be using 'grounding' after training.   At six months follow-up however, the difference in use of tokens disappeared, and a rather unexpected result occurred, namely that those in the control group were more likely to report themselves as using strategies which are best categorised as 'response cost'.

1.5 The hypothesis that children in the experimental group would have fewer unplanned terminations of placements in which behaviour problems were implicated was not supported.

1.6 Generally, carers in the training group did not use behavioural terminology when describing the strategies they used to manage behaviour, despite their increased knowledge of behavioural principles.

1.7 Participants in the training programme did not report a significant reduction in the range of problems that they found particularly difficult or challenging, compared with foster carers in the wait-list control (Hypothesis 4). There were no differences between the two groups at any time point.

1.8 Foster carers in the training programme did not report more success than those in the control group in dealing with behaviour problems (Hypothesis 5). However, particular caution is required when interpreting these data as we secured few completed Child Behaviour Checklists, on which these results primarily depend. Data from the Course Task and from qualitative data provided during the interviews suggest that carers in the training programme are both using these techniques and having success where they themselves would otherwise not have expected success. These data are reviewed and discussed in Chapter 6.

6. Foster Carers' Use of Behavioural Methods (Chapter 6)

1.1 Evidence from the records kept by foster carers indicates a secure basis in behavioural analysis, but weakness in the use of cognitive-behavioural interventions.

1.2 The conclusions drawn from these data and the trainers' experience of running the training programme are (i) that the programme needs to ensure that participants understand the principles underpinning behavioural interventions, (ii) that they have a firm understanding of how to use them appropriately and effectively, and (iii) that the programme provides more opportunities to practice their implementation, both in the training situation and at home.

1.3 These aspects were essential components of the programme, but the size of the group, poor attendance, and the challenges facing carers meant that this aspect of training was often 'squeezed'. In addition, few carers routinely completed the homework assignments, which were a key component of the course.

7. Foster Carer Satisfaction (Chapter 7)

1.1 With the exception of one or two participants, satisfaction with the programme was generally very high. All but seven of the respondents said they were either satisfied (25) or very satisfied (16) with the training they had received.

1.2 Most respondents reported improvements in the behaviour problems that had prompted them to participate in training.

1.3 The majority of carers thought that their child's behaviour had improved in general since participating in the course, and most were satisfied with the degree of progress. All but nine foster carers saw the training programme as having helped bring about these improvements.

1.4 Over 82% indicated that they felt very positively about the future, and all but five said they would 'recommend' (n=20) or 'strongly recommend' (n=23) the programme to other carers.

8. Discussion (Chapter 8)

1.1 We should be rightly suspicious of attempts explain away results, but it is also negligent to disregard lessons learned and plausible explanations for why a particular pattern of results have fallen as they have.

1.2 Certain lessons learned in the course of the training, and in the conduct of the study, urge caution in concluding that training in cognitive-behavioural methods is not an effective means of helping carers to manage difficult behaviour or to prevent unplanned terminations of placement. There is much here to support the view that training foster carers in cognitive behavioural skills is an appropriate undertaking, but that it may require more than a short course.

1.3 Essentially, the current study points to the need to make certain changes in the training provided in order to maximise (or perhaps to ensure) its impact. These are essentially to provide a longer training programme, to limit the size of the groups, and to find a way of improving / securing full attendance and completing homework. This should enable an appropriate emphasis to be maintained on developing the skills of cognitive-behavioural interventions, as well as cognitive-behavioural analysis. Some carers might do better on a one-to-one basis, at least initially, as some appeared to struggle in the group context.

1.4 Many of the children's Scores on the Child Well-being Checklist fell within the clinical range (for Total Scores, and Sub-scales), and many more were in the borderline range. Often the carers were concerned about problems that were clearly 'clinical' in nature e.g. attention deficit hyperactivity disorder, conduct disorder, and we were obliged to direct them to expert help. For these children, behaviour management is necessary but not sufficient. It is not surprising that insofar as the behaviour problems that carers were facing were the manifestation of much more substantial difficulties, the study showed no differences in the rates of placement breakdown (see also below).

1.5 Some carers pointed to the need for 'on the spot' advice, or easy access to help. The idea of a 'problem clinic' was suggested, and generally welcomed by group members.

9. Conclusions (Chapter 9) 1.1 This evaluation suggests that the programme was not effective in achieving a number of its aims. There are, however, indications that this might have been attributable, at least in part, to (i) some organisational difficulties which impacted upon the strength of the study to address those aims, (ii) limitations in the length and effective content of the programme, and (iii) a lack of available support within the agencies to help foster carers implement newly acquired skills. In terms of their perceived need for such training, their overall satisfaction with the programme, and the evidence from Course Tasks, the programme was seen as a significant source of advice, knowledge and skills development. Many carers commented that the programme should be a requirement of all new foster carers.

1.2 An appropriate 'next step' would be to revise the programme in line with the preceding recommendations and make this available to the control group, and their progress monitored. The revisions are discussed in more detail in chapter 9.

Chapter one

Introduction

This chapter sets the context for the study. It begins with a brief summary of the situation in England and Wales with regard to children looked after. It then outlines the evidence underpinning the rationale for the study, and concludes with a statement of the study's aims and objectives.

Children Looked After

Since 1994 the number of children looked after at any one time has hovered at the 80,000 mark (DH 2002). The number of children looked after by English local authorities who have been looked after continuously for at least one year increased from 42,200 to 43,400 between 2002-2003. Children looked after for more than six months have increased significantly, from around 60,000 in 1994 to 70,000 in 2001. This increase is most marked for children aged 3 or under.

Outcomes for Children Looked After

At the end of March 2001 65% of all looked after children were living with foster carers and 6% were placed for adoption (DH 2001). These figures are higher for younger children under ten years of age.

Whilst there is much to celebrate in the substantial shift away from residential or institutional care towards care in substitute families, children looked after continue consistently to fare less well than others on a range of indicators, including health, education, and social adjustment. One of the factors that increases children's risks of adverse outcomes is lack of placement stability. Disruptions to placements and frequent changes of carers can undermine children's capacity for developing meaningful attachments, disrupt friendships, and contribute to discontinuities in education and health.

Table 1.1 (overleaf) summarises the profile of children in the South West of England experiencing three or more placement moves in one year since 1997, and sets this in the overall national context. For about half the local authorities in this region the percentage of children experiencing three or more placements in one year was reducing at the end of March 2001.

The remainder were evidencing slight trends upwards.

Increasing placement stability

In 1999 local authorities were set a target of reducing to no more than 16% the number of children who experience three or more moves during one year (DH 2001). This required that local authorities appraise the factors contributing to foster placement breakdown, and find ways of addressing those that fell within their influence. In large part this has resulted in local authorities looking at ways of better supporting foster carers and the children they look after on their behalf.

Table 1.1 Children looked after at 31 March 1997-2001, with three or more placements during the year.[1,2,3]

Numbers and percentages of all looked after children at 31 March 2001

	numbers						percentages[4]				
National	10,000	10,400	10,500	10,800	9,600		**20**	**19**	**19**	**19**	**16**
South West											
Shire Counties[5]	**1997**	**1998**	**1999**	**2000**	**2001**		**1997**	**1998**	**1999**	**2000**	**2001**
Cornwall	151	176	119	84	83		31	33	22	15	14
Devon	91	82	67	93	101		15	14	10	13	14
Dorset	87	80	50	37	24		28	29	20	14	10
Gloucestershire	52	94	115	86	94		13	20	23	17	17
Somerset	100	94	88	91	100		25	23	24	27	30
Wiltshire	45	41	65	52	52		17	16	25	20	20
Unitary Authorities	**1997**	**1998**	**1999**	**2000**	**2001**		**1997**	**1998**	**1999**	**2000**	**2001**
Bath and NE Somerset	19	23	18	35	20		13	18	13	24	14
Bournemouth	58	49	38	55	79		36	25	21	27	38
Bristol	82	151	77	121	81		15	26	14	22	14
North Somerset	40	47	42	46	29		28	32	30	30	18
Plymouth	57	26	33	57	56		16	8	9	14	12
Poole	43	37	19	56	27		34	34	16	39	30
South Gloucestershire	19	40	37	36	35		13	23	23	26	25
Swindon	50	26	38	38	65		26	16	20	21	40
Torbay	25	29	42	20	29		16	14	19	8	12

[1] Taken from http://www.doh.gov.uk/public/cla2001.htm.

[2] Figures for 1998-2001 are estimated from the SSDA "one third" sample and are therefore subject to sampling error. Some caution is therefore needed when making comparisons at the LA level, particularly when the number of children involved is small (See Technical Notes in source).

[3] Exclude agreed series of short-term placements. All other placements recorded on the SSDA903 are included (see Section 2 of Commentary in source for further explanation).

[4] Percentages represent indicator A1 of the Performance Assessment Framework.

[5] Excludes Scilly Isles.

Local authorities in the South West are concerned to promote an evidence-based approach to policy and practice. This project, commissioned by the Centre for Evidence-Based Social Services, was designed to help take forward this agenda. All but one of the participating authorities was already meeting government targets, some more comfortably than others. Only one of the authorities not meeting these targets was involved in the study. Clearly, concerns other than placement stability contributed to participation, including concerns about supporting foster carers.

Causes of unplanned endings to placement

Children looked after have long been recognised as experiencing high rates of behavioural and emotional problems (see George 1970; Rowe and Lambert 1973; Keane 1983; Rowe et al. 1984; Thoburn and Rowe 1991). They experience substantially higher levels of mental health problems than children in the general population (McCann et al. 1996) and the incidence of behaviour problems remains particularly high (Dimigen et al. 1999). For some children, their behavioural and emotional disturbances have contributed directly to the decisions to accommodate them (see Milham et al. 1986; Packman et al. 1986). For others, their behavioural problems reflect unhelpful ways of responding to, or coping with, a variety of other factors, such as rejection, abuse, neglect, mental health problems, and so on. As the profile of children looked-after has changed, the incidence and prevalence of these difficulties has increased significantly (Thorpe 1980; Triseliotis 1987; Thomas and Beckett 1994; Warren 1997).

Among the many reasons why behaviour problems are important is that they are strongly correlated with the unplanned termination of placement (Parker 1966; George 1970; Napier 1972; Aldgate and Hawley 1986; Borland et al. 1991; DH 1991). It is increasingly acknowledged that the term 'placement breakdown' does not do justice to the complexities of the issues involved when placements end prematurely. The term is used in this report however, albeit recognising that it is not always the best descriptor. Berridge and Cleaver found that behaviour problems in very young children in short-term placements could threaten placement stability:

> Investigation of case notes revealed that children, even those who were very young, could pose considerable problems for short-term foster parents and temper tantrums, excessive swings in mood, attention-seeking behaviour and other signs of emotional disturbance were not uncommon … indeed, as our analysis reveals, the primary reasons for the breakdown of 30% of placements were essentially 'child-focused'.

> *Berridge and Cleaver 1987: 115*

With each placement breakdown, children are likely to experience more rejection and to develop ever more defensive ways of managing an unpredictable world. They are less likely readily to establish intimate relationships with subsequent carers, and more likely to exhibit behaviours which keep carers (and others) at arms' length. Such maladaptive attempts at self-protection increase the risk of problems developing within the placement, and often children's challenging behaviour leads to a self-fulfilling prophecy – more rejection. Concerns about this particular cycle underpin the government's objective of ensuring that children who cannot be cared for in their family of origin 'are securely attached to carers capable of providing safe and effective care for the duration of childhood'. Such secure attachment is also important because of other things that it protects against. Frequent moves increase the likelihood that children will lose friendships, have to adjust to new schools, and so on. Minimising the numbers of placements experienced by children looked after is therefore an important objective, and one in which the ability of foster carers to manage challenging behaviour (both in terms of 'coping' and of effecting changes in) assumes considerable significance.

Foster carers' needs

Berridge and Cleaver also note that whilst many foster parents evince impressive tolerance and coping in the face of such behavioural and emotional onslaughts, that many are 'clearly unprepared for the sorts of demands that severely emotionally deprived children would make on them' (Berridge and Cleaver 1987: 63). Seven years later, Nissim and Simm highlighted behavioural problems as one of four characteristics of children and young people that were linked to either a positive or negative outcome. They recommended serious attention is paid to this area, because:

> When there are up to a dozen studies conducted over a thirty year period which all point in the same direction, we have to take what they say very seriously. More than that, we have a responsibility to translate this evidence into our daily practice.
>
> *Nissim and Simm 1994: 13*

Despite this long-established body of evidence, little has been done to prepare and support foster carers for the challenges they face. Child behavioural difficulties and foster carers' lack of confidence in dealing with these (see below) continue to feature in research (Sinclair et al. 2000).

Training and support

In recent years increasing attention has been paid to the careful selection and preparation of foster carers. Since the late 1960s, foster carer training programs have proliferated, and hundreds of unpublished curricula have been developed by individual and private child welfare agencies (cf. Zukoski 1999). They use numerous formats and a broad range of training methods (Berry 1988). Foster carers generally are trained in groups, with training broadly aimed at meeting the needs of foster carers who will be caring for children of all ages. In general, there are two types of foster carer training. One is skill-based training, which provides information to promote the typical developmental needs of children and child management techniques. The other type focuses on providing foster carers with information and support to assist them in understanding their roles and responsibilities and reinforcing their efforts as they encounter the variety of issues associated with being a foster parent (Hampson 1985). Lee and Holland (1991) found that 'the content of many fostering training efforts often include attention to three broad areas: (a) understanding child development and preparing for anticipated difficulties between child and parents, (b) orientation of foster parents to the agency and community services available to them, (c) support for the functioning of the foster family in order to increase placement stability' (p. 163).

Some training programmes now being implemented are targeted particularly at managing problem behaviour using non-aversive techniques. These are essentially strategies for managing or containing crisis situations without resource to physical strategies that could either harm the young people concerned, or leave foster carers vulnerable to complaint or prosecution e.g. SCIP[6]). Few of these programmes have been evaluated and the range of behaviour problems that fracture foster placements is much wider and more complex in its effects (Nissim and Simm 1994).

The trends in placement breakdowns – though always a complex phenomenon – do not suggest that current practices are succeeding in better equipping foster carers to manage the very considerable challenges presented by children with serious behavioural and emotional problems. This may be because these programmes are too general in nature.

There is no doubt that foster carers value general support, but they also value expert and timely advice in relation to particular difficulties. For example, in a survey of the views of 109 foster carers in one local authority, serious behaviour problems were noted by 40% of respondents, and such problems were identified as directly contributing to placement breakdown in the previous five years. Of the 58% who had attended training provided by the Social Services Department concerned, three-quarters said they found this useful. However, the majority of foster carers said that training needed to be better developed, to be offered more regularly (and at more convenient times), and that easy access to expert advice regarding specific placement difficulties would be beneficial (Romero 1995).

Similarly, Quinton et al. (1998) reported that foster carers often cited a need for help targeted specifically at enabling them to manage difficult behaviour.

This project was designed to test whether training foster carers in methods designed to help people to manage challenging behaviour would have benefits for looked-after children and foster carers. We were primarily concerned to test whether it enabled carers better to manage difficult behaviour, but we were also interested in whether it would help them feel more confident in their capacity to care for challenging children and young people, and, ultimately, whether improved skills and/or confidence would enhance placement stability.

[6] 'Strategies for Crisis Intervention and Prevention', New York Office of Mental Retardation and Development Disabilities.

INTRODUCTION

5

Chapter two

Managing Challenging Behaviour

This chapter summarises the basis on which the training programme was developed. The conceptual and empirical basis of the training rests (i) on evidence regarding effective strategies for helping parents develop their parenting skills in general, and their skills in managing child behaviour in particular; and (ii) on what is known about the effectiveness of interventions designed to manage behaviour problems that fall outside the range of 'normal' child behaviour problems.

What works in behaviour management?

Parent training

There is now an extensive body of research examining the effectiveness of a range of interventions designed to help parents better manage children's behaviour. This research, on what is generically referred to as 'parent training', has been extensively reviewed (Cedar 1990; Todres 1993; Barlow 1997) with some encouraging findings (see Barlow 1999, for a rigorous, systematic review). In brief, the findings of individual studies, and reviews, favour group-based behavioural or cognitive-behavioural programmes. Barlow's conclusion is typical:

> Overall …. behavioural group-based parent-training programmes appear to produce better results when compared with Parent Effectiveness Training (PET) and Adlerian programmes. This confirms the findings of [earlier] overviews.
>
> *Barlow 1997: 32*

Effective interventions for serious behaviour problems

Clearly, the task of parenting – whilst challenging – is rather different to that of looking after children who have been removed from their families of origin. The reasons for children becoming looked after are varied, but rarely minor in their nature or potential consequences. Extended efforts to maintain a family unit may have resulted in children being exposed to maltreatment for a considerable time, or to less than optimal parenting as a result of substance misuse, mental illness, chaotic lifestyles, and so on. By the time children become looked after, many will not only have had to face a series of difficulties but will have developed emotional and behavioural problems as a result of those difficulties and adverse experiences. What might be effective in terms of managing 'simple' behaviour problems might be less effective in dealing with more serious ones.

When children's behaviour problems are severe and persistent, resulting in serious impairment of functioning, they are usually referred to as conduct disordered. Without labelling children looked after as conduct disordered, it is the case that the extent and severity of their behaviour problems often exceeds that of the general population. It is therefore pertinent to consider what is known about effective help for children whose problems are more serious than those with which most parents routinely deal. One source of such information is to examine the evidence of 'what works' with children who have conduct disorders.

Even in this context the research evidence about 'what works' remains the same, with cognitive-behavioural approaches faring well in comparison with others (see Serketich and Dumas 1996; Brestan and Eyberg 1998; Bennett and Gibbons 2000; Wolfenden et al. 2000; van de Wiel 2002).

The reasons for the effectiveness of cognitive-behavioural methods relative to other approaches is perhaps because of the 'logical fit' between the way that problems are conceptualised and the strategies designed to address them. Cognitive-behavioural approaches have their conceptual and empirical bases in the learning theories, particularly social learning theory.

Social learning theory

Essentially, social learning theory highlights the ways in which a major part of our behavioural and emotional repertoires are learned. In this model, learning does not need to be either intentional or conscious. Rather, we develop ways of thinking, feeling and behaviour as a result of our interactions with our environment, particularly our social environment. For example, children learn to be compliant, agreeable, and self-controlled by a complex and sustained pattern of interaction with parents and significant others. For the most part this process of socialisation happens naturally rather than in any particularly 'planful' way. Sometimes though, as when particular difficulties emerge, parents or teachers have to think more strategically. Also, because we mainly socialise our children on 'auto-pilot', there is always the possibility that the very processes we use can inadvertently shape unwanted behaviours. Modelling, for example, is a very powerful means of acquiring new patterns of behaviour, and young children can easily model aggression as a means of coping with stress, or solving problems. It is very easy to reinforce unwanted behaviour by attending to it. Attention itself, even when intended to communicate disapproval, can – for some children in some circumstances – be reinforcing.

Cognition is also an important factor in social learning theory. What children think about themselves and others is also a function of experience and learning. What we think inevitably influences how we respond to our environments. Children who have been abused or neglected, or otherwise subjected to environments that have impacted badly upon them, are likely to internalise these experiences. They may well attribute to themselves the responsibility for what has happened to them – or to their carers. They may learn that the world is an unpredictable place, over which they have no influence. Therefore, they may find it hard to believe that 'trying harder' will make a difference, or that these carers really do care. It is important, therefore, for foster carers to have a good understanding of the child's situation, and to be sensitive to his or her feelings and attributions (see Hampson and Tavormina 1980). Without these skills they are unlikely to be able correctly to understand a child's behaviour or to develop appropriate and effective helping strategies.

Cognitive-behavioural approaches

Cognitive-behavioural approaches essentially comprise a careful analysis of the antecedents and consequences of challenging behaviour (including the impact of early experiences, temperament and so on) and – on the basis of that analysis – developing a programme designed to facilitate and reinforce change. Typically, it entails helping participants to develop (i) an understanding of the ways in which behaviour can be shaped by the environment; (ii) skills in analysing behaviour – commonly referred to as the ABC of behaviour[7]; (iii) selecting strategies to change the relationship between behaviour and its consequences and/or changing the antecedents (e.g. asking a child to get ready for bed after making it clear what his/her bedtime is and turning the television off before asking); and (iv) monitoring and reviewing progress.

Foster carers are generally competent parents, and therefore probably intuitive behaviourists, but they rarely have access, especially in the UK, to training in cognitive-behavioural approaches. Participation in an appropriately designed training programme should improve carers' understanding of the factors contributing to the development and maintenance of behaviour problems (the basic ABC approach) and enable them to identify and deploy effectively appropriate techniques. The end result should be one or more of the following: a) an increase in knowledge of behavioural problems and how to

[7] Where 'A' represents 'antecedents,' 'B' represents 'behaviour' and 'C' represents 'consequences.

manage them (in cognitive-behavioural terms), b) an increase in skills in the management of behaviour problems, c) an increase in confidence in carers' perceived ability to cope with/manage children with behavioural problems, and d) a decrease in behavioural problems (or their frequency or severity). Insofar as behaviour problems are the precipitating cause of placement breakdown, successful participation in cognitive-behavioural training should result in increased placement stability (a decrease in the frequency of unplanned terminations of placement). At the time the study was initiated there were only a few studies available that had explored the effectiveness of training foster carers in behavioural or cognitive behavioural methods. Table 2.1 provides an overview of these studies.

Only 17 studies of the effectiveness of training, using a variety of study designs, appear to have been conducted since 1977. All but two are American (and at the time this study commenced, the only published reports were American), and not all comprise rigorous evaluations i.e. evaluations with at least a control group. Many authors note a range of difficulties in conducting high quality evaluations.

Studies are evaluating a range of training programmes, using a range of comparisons (when comparison groups are used at all) and widely different outcome measures. This, together with the problems noted makes it difficult to draw firm conclusions from such an overview. Taken together, however, the studies suggest the potential of cognitive-behavioural training programmes as a means of helping foster carers in their endeavours to manage and influence difficult behaviour. Since the study began, two UK studies have been published (Hill-Tout et al. 2001; Pallet et al. 2002), only one of which used a control group. One of these reports very positive findings, but did not deploy a control group and relied on post-test data (Pallett et al. 2001). Further, it used outcome measures that were rejected in this study as inappropriate (because they were developed and standardised for birth parents, for example). Hill-Tout et al. did use a control group and collected data before and after the programme. We discuss both studies in more detail later.

Table 2.1 Studies of the effectiveness of foster carer training programmes

Authors	Date	Study Design	Intervention	Results
Guerney	1977	PTPT 2G[8]	Parenting Skills Programme (Group)	Trained carers showed marked improvement relative to controls: more accepting attitudes toward children, able to employ desirable parenting responses and refrain from undesirable ones.
Katz	1977	PTPT 3G[9]	Gordon's Parent Effectiveness Training (PET)	Participants in PET evidenced significant improvement on the Hereford Parent Attitude Survey compared with a topical discussion group and a no-treatment control group.
Boyd & Remy	1978	Quasi-exp	Pre-service, behaviour oriented, training (16 weeks)	Training reduced the incidence of failed placements, increased the probability of desirable placement outcomes, and increased the probability of foster parents remaining licensed.
Penn	1978	Group case study	Pre-placement behaviour training (11 weeks)	Completed Child Behaviour Inventories on 15 children of seven carers involved in the study indicated that 131 specific behaviours improved and 27 deteriorated during the duration of the training. Improvements and deterioration were noted for both natural and foster children. The eight natural children who were observed improved on an average 4.8 behaviours and deteriorated on 1.25 behaviours. An average 13 instances of positive and 2.5 cases of negative change were reported for the seven foster children in the study. As there was no comparison group, the results of this study are, to a large extent, uninterpretable.
Brown	1980	RCT	Compared a Foster Parent Skills Training Program (FPSTP) with a discussion group (Issues in Fostering) and with a 'no contact' control	No differences between the training groups and 'no contact' control group on parental attitudes, but a difference favouring FPSTP with respect to sensitivity to children when compared to the IF programme. However, the author highlights serious problems with attrition, possible lack of equivalence between the groups, and limitations of the measures.
Hampson & Tavormina	1980	RCT	Compared reflective training model (emphasised parental awareness, understanding and acceptance of children's feelings) with behavioural model	Participants in each group showed positive changes in the domain emphasised in their respective training approach and little change in the other domain. Researchers concluded that foster parent training should incorporate both types of training to ensure foster parent effectiveness across a broad range of conditions.
Levant & Geer	1981	Quasi-exp	Training in helping and communication-oriented parenting skills versus no training for carers selected for their high levels of empathy, warmth and genuineness	No significant differences were found with respect to foster child's self-esteem, behaviour adjustment or placement stability. No significant improvement in helping and parenting skills were obtained. Authors consider the results to be attributable to difficulties encountered by the participants in their daily lives that interfered with the instructional plan.

[8] Pre-test Post-test two group (Intervention Group, Waiting list group who could not attend sessions).

[9] Pre-test Post-test three group design (Intervention, Discussion Group, Control Group).

Table 2.1 continued Studies of the effectiveness of foster carer training programmes

Authors	Date	Study Design	Intervention	Results
Cobb, Leitenberg & Burchard	1982	Quasi-exp	Training in communication and conflict resolution skills	Trained carers differed significantly on measures assessing communication and problems solving compared with control group carers, based on audio-taped recorded responses to stimulus situations.
Simon & Simon	1982	One-group, historical control.	NOVA (Nova University's Foster Parent Project) that encompassed foster carer recruitment, selection and training	Combining a pre-service training programme with a home study process significantly increased the number of licensed families. Trained foster parents accepted twice the number of placements and had 50% fewer disruptions of placement than the control group. They were also more likely to accept children who were considered 'high risk' placements.
Hampson, Shulte & Ricks	1983	Quasi-exp	Behavioural and reflective methods, provided either in a group environment or in the carers' home	Both groups showed improvements in attitude scores and in the knowledge and use of behavioural principles. Those trained in their homes did better than those trained in groups on the following measures: parents' attendance rates, ratings of child behaviour improvement and scoring of satisfaction with family functioning at the end of training.
Dutes	1985	PTPT 2G	Compared 2 behaviourally oriented foster carer training and self-management, the other only child behaviour management	The two groups did not differ significantly on the outcome measures. The author suggests that selection bias (due to attrition) poor attendance, insufficient training time, participants' inadequate reading and writing skills, and trainers' inexperience of low educational levels, offered competing explanations of the results.
Lee & Holland	1991	PTPT comparison	MAPP: emphasises (a) rights and obligations of carers, (b) shared decision making among carers, agency staff and birth parents and (c) mutual selection of carers by agency and agency by foster carers. Programme aims to develop knowledge, attitudes, knowledge and skills necessary to be effective and satisfied foster carers	No statistically significant differences on any measures used. The authors attribute this inconsistency with previous research to methodological inadequacies/differences.

Table 2.1 continued Studies of the effectiveness of foster carer training programmes

Authors	Date	Study Design	Intervention	Results
Chamberlain Moreland & Reid	1992	RCT	Carers were randomly assigned to either: • Enhanced staff contact and training plus an increase in monthly stipend • Increased monthly stipend • Neither of the above	Study demonstrated the positive effect of increased stipends and enhanced training and support on minimising foster carer drop-out rates.
Burry	1999	PTPT –2G	Multi-modal in-service training programme designed to enhance the competency and intent of foster carers to care for infants with prenatal substance effects	Results showed that only the foster carers' skills and knowledge increased at post-test. The training goals for increasing efficacy, social support, and intent to foster were not achieved.
Hill-Tout et al.	2001	Quasi-exp[10]	Group training combining positive parenting skills development to promote positive alternatives to inappropriate conduct, (b) ecological interface – smoothing the fit between individual and environment, and (c) reactive strategies – dealing with emergencies.	No significant differences occurred in number of exclusions from community facilities, number and frequency of presenting behaviours, or carers' emotional response. There were some significant differences in some sub-scales with the intervention group giving more credence to emotional and bio-medical factors, but no significant differences across total scores. There were no between-group differences in carer stress, or carer capacity to identify a range of variables across challenging behaviour or to demonstrate insight into their own responses.
Pallett et al.	2002	PTPT 1G[11]	Group cognitive-behavioural training	Authors report significant improvements in carer-child interaction, child difficulty and specific child problems causing most worry to carers, and child emotional symptoms. Insignificant improvements were seen in hyperactivity and conduct problems. There is some doubt about the suitability of some of the measures used in this study, however.

[10] There is insufficient information at the time of writing to be certain of the methodology. This may have been a randomised controlled trial.

[11] Pre-test Post-test One Group Design.

The study   Within social care in the UK, behavioural methods were for a long time largely eschewed as overly mechanistic and concerned with 'symptoms' rather than underlying causes. This perhaps explains why it is only very recently that such approaches have gained some currency. The enhanced focus on thoughts and feelings in cognitive-behavioural approaches has gone some way to attenuate these concerns. Further, the growth in evidence regarding their effectiveness across a wide range of psychological problems has made their rejection appear particularly eccentric at a time when evidence-based policy and practice are being advocated and espoused.

The lack of enthusiasm for behavioural and even cognitive-behavioural approaches is, however, also a consequence of other factors. Two of these have a bearing on foster care. First, there remain differences of view about the nature of social and psychological problems, and where it is appropriate to intervene. There are often concerns in social work in particular that a focus on the level of the individual ignores the impact of structural factors and inappropriately labels people as the problem. As with other causes for concern, this is at least in part attributable to misunderstanding about the nature and complexity of cognitive-behavioural approaches. This is not to say that such approaches have not been applied in mechanistic ways, or indeed misused e.g. used for the smooth running of institutions, rather than the well-being of those cared for. Most advocates of cognitive-behavioural approaches would, however, argue that the effective and ethical application of these strategies depends on a sound understanding of human development and of the nature of problems such as conduct disorder, anxiety, depression, and so on. Many cognitive-behavioural programmes, including those used to help children looked after, are broadly based, deploying social learning theory to analyse and intervene in a range of systems e.g. school, community, and health service (see Macdonald 2001).

Secondly, with the exception of psychologists and mental health nurses, few professionals are taught the skills and knowledge required to implement these approaches. If family placement workers, social workers, health visitors and teachers do not have a grounding in social learning theory then the odds are stacked against the successful resolution of many child behaviour problems. It also raises important issues regarding the sustainability of skills when teaching is provided. This is an issue we return to later.

Study Aims

At the time this study was commissioned, cognitive-behavioural methods had begun to make their presence felt in a number of arenas, including probation, clinical psychology and mental health. Their effectiveness in helping parents manage a wide range of behaviour problems was established. This study sought to investigate the effectiveness of training foster carers in such management skills. Specifically, it wanted to explore the extent to which such training would:

(i)   enable foster carers more effectively to manage the behaviour problems presented by children in their care;

(ii)   lead to greater placement stability.

We were also interested to explore what level and kind of support foster carers might require in order to develop and maintain behaviour management skills in what are often difficult circumstances.

Study Hypotheses   Our hypotheses were as follows:

(i)   *Participants in the training programme condition would score significantly higher on the Knowledge of Behavioural Principles as Applied to Children (KBPAC) (O'Dell, Tarler-Benlolo & Flynn 1979) scale than foster carers in the wait-list control condition.*[12]

We anticipated that the training programme, whilst not didactic in nature (see next chapter), would equip foster carers with an understanding of behavioural principles and behavioural strategies. The measure used is designed specifically to test this in relation to child management.

(ii)   *Participants in the training programme would be significantly more likely than foster carers in the wait-list control group to use behavioural techniques in managing children's behaviour.*

We expected foster carers to incorporate the strategies they learned, including ABC analysis, into the ways in which they responded to challenging behaviour, and in their general approach to child management. The programme included homework assignments that we thought would build confidence, highlight areas for clarification and development, and provide reinforcement for the use of these approaches.

(iii)   *For children in the experimental group*[13] *there would be fewer unplanned terminations of placement in which behaviour problems were implicated.*

[12] Those foster carers who were randomly assigned to the control group.

[13] The 'training group'.

This was perhaps our riskiest hypothesis. We recognised that the training programme was relatively brief compared with others (see Pallett et al. 2001) and that there was not an infrastructure in place to help foster carers in the day-to-day implementation of the knowledge and skills they might acquire. Further, behaviour problems are only one of a constellation of factors that contribute to unplanned terminations of placement. Nonetheless, this was the acid test of the potential effectiveness of this intervention.

(iv) *Participants in the training programme would report a significant reduction in the range of problems that they found particularly difficult or challenging, compared with foster carers in the wait-list control.*

We anticipated that the training would enable carers successfully to tackle problems they had previously found difficult to manage. As above, we thought that training would help foster carers better to manage difficult behaviour, even if this did not result in increased placement stability.

(v) *Foster carers in the training programme would report success in dealing with behaviour problems.*

We hoped that not only would foster carers be more likely to use cognitive-behavioural methods, but that they would do so successfully.

(vi) *Foster carers would feel more confident in their abilities to manage difficult behaviour.*

Research testifies to foster carers' sense of isolation and lack of confidence in their abilities to manage what are, after all, very difficult emotional and behavioural problems. We thought that by enhancing their understanding of how such behaviours develop, and how one might intervene, that carers who had participated in the training would feel more secure in their dealings with children. They would be less likely to misattribute challenging behaviour (for example, taking things personally) and their ability to analyse and understand behaviour would promote a sense of self-efficacy and control.

Chapter three

The Training Programme

This chapter provides some information about the training programme, its content and delivery, and expectations placed on participants.

Content

The content of the training programme developed for this study mirrors that of programmes that have proved effective when provided to groups of parents facing difficulties with their children (e.g. Webster-Stratton 1998). It was planned in collaboration with one of the two trainers, Martin Herbert. Professor Herbert generously allowed us to draw heavily on his earlier work, and that of his colleague J Wookey, with parenting groups for birth parents. The programme manual mirrors that prepared for these groups (see Herbert and Wookey, in press).

Social learning theory

The training sought to familiarise carers with an understanding of social learning theory, both in terms of how behaviour develops and how it can be influenced using interventions derived from social learning theory. There was an emphasis throughout on developing the skills to observe, describe and analyse behaviour in behavioural terms – the so-called 'ABC' analysis. In the programme, these skills were developed before moving on to consider specific strategies or interventions, though in reality the way in which the training was conducted resulted in some fluidity between sessions (see below). The trainers made sure that all aspects of the programme were covered, using an inventory which was completed at the end of each session.

The fostering context

Fostering does not happen in a vacuum and we thought it important to address the context in which fostering occurs, both from the point of view of the impact of fostering on carers and their families, but also from the point of view of the child.

Fostering is a difficult job and foster carers are subject to a variety of pressures (see Wilson et al. 2000). Some of these pressures arise from the policy and regulatory frameworks within which they work, and which necessarily impact upon what they are able to do. It was important to ensure that the programme did not add to these pressures, and that there was a 'match' between what was being taught and what was realistic from the carers' perspectives. Some mismatches that caused concern to both carers and trainers are dealt with in the discussion.

In relation to the children, the training programme sought to ensure that each child's particular situation was taken into account. To some extent this arises naturally when one considers the child's history (i.e. distal antecedents) but we thought it important formally to include something on attachment theory too. This is an important contextual factor influencing both a child's behaviour and what it might be appropriate (or inappropriate) to do when faced with a problem that needs to be resolved. Many foster carers had received training on attachment theory, and attachment disorders, and we were not seeking to replicate this. Rather, we were concerned to ensure that participants understood how early experiences contribute to emotional, behavioural and psychological development, and did not leave the programme thinking that a cognitive-behavioural approach was simply a 'tool-kit' approach in which 'off the shelf interventions' were available for use. The effective and ethical application of cognitive-behavioural methods requires as a starting point a good understanding of the nature of the problems, how they have come about, and their function. For children looked after, their attachment histories are a significant variable in informing both assessment and choice of intervention.

Self-efficacy or 'can do'

It is sometimes the case that the reason people do not respond appropriately in stressful situations is not attributable to lack of skills, or insight into how best to handle a situation (Meichenbaum and Turk 1982). Rather, it is because of a lack of belief in one's ability to act or to bring about change. In other words, people sometimes lack confidence in their abilities to tackle problems, or do not think they can succeed, even if they try. The curriculum was therefore designed to promote a sense of confidence or self-efficacy (Bandura 1982) on the part of foster carers. It did this essentially by encouraging foster carers to apply behavioural and cognitive behavioural principles to an analysis of their own learning and their own responses to situations, and by affirming and reinforcing their endeavours.

Foster carers were helped to tune into cognitions that negatively affected their appraisal of foster children's behaviours via discussions of beliefs, values and attitudes that underlie perceptions of problematic behaviours. Carers were encouraged to recognise how such cognitions affected their ability to parent foster children through their effects on their own behaviour. It was emphasised that since much behaviour is learned, foster children can be helped to 'unlearn' maladaptive behaviours and acquire new, prosocial ways of behaving. Foster carers were encouraged to see challenging behaviour not as catastrophic, but as a problem to be solved.

In keeping with Meichenbaum's (1977) proposition that individuals can instruct themselves how to behave differently in stressful situations, foster carers were encouraged to develop a positive self-image about their ability to help a child to find new, appropriate ways of behaving. Part of this strategy entailed teaching carers to take time to step back from a situation, consider it calmly, and to analyse it carefully. This reflects evidence that the greater a person's ability to anticipate or engage in stressful situations in a calm and controlled manner, the more confident he or she is likely to feel about his/her ability to handle such situations (Bandura 1982), and the more likely he or she is to succeed.

Organisation The programme was originally designed as five weekly, three-hour sessions plus a follow-up session. This was the format used for the first two groups, and was the form in which the pilot was conducted. The pilot group comprised some eight carers. The groups that comprised the intervention groups were much larger. Partly because of the size of these groups (see next chapter), and the very participative nature of the programme, we found that these sessions were rather 'packed' e.g. when we needed to elicit information from each participant it took quite a long time. We therefore decided to move to four weekly, five-hour sessions plus a follow-up for the remaining four groups. The content of the programme remained unchanged. The programme for these four longer sessions is outlined in Table 3.1. At the end of each programme a follow-up day was arranged with participants. This was primarily designed as an opportunity for participants to come together to discuss their experiences of implementing these interventions over a period of time, and to present their work (see below).

Table 3.1 Outline of Training Programme

Session 1.
- Rationale of the research
- Rationale underpinning the training
- Problems and Expectations
- Identifying target problems
- The problem-solving approach
- Describing in behavioural terms
- The importance of observation
- ABC of behaviour

Session 2.
- Reviewing homework
- The social context of child care
  - *social learning theory / attachment theory /typologies of attachment*
- The fostering task
  - *special dilemmas for fostering another person's child*
  - *the impact on the family/household*
- Assessing challenging behaviour
  - *ABC analysis*
  - *learning theory*
  - *understanding the impact of a child's learning history.*
- Assessment exercise

Session 3.
- Reviewing homework
- Change strategies
  - *How do we influence people in general?*
  - *What strategies can we use to influence an adult in our midst?*
  - *What strategies can we use to influence looked-after children?*
  - *What can't we use?*
  - *What can go wrong? What works for you?*
  - *Positive parenting*
  - *Discipline as leadership*
- Behavioural strategies 1:
  Strategies for increasing desired behaviour
  - *Goal setting*
  - *'I' messages*
  - *Positive reinforcement*
  - *Quality time*
  - *Grandma's rule*
- Making decisions
- Behavioural strategies 2:
  Strategies for decreasing undesired behaviour
  - *Time out*
  - *Logical consequences*
  - *Response cost*
  - *Reinforcing incompatible responses*
  - *Negotiating and contracting*

Table 3.1 continued - Outline of Training Programme

Session 4.
- Reviewing homework
- Creating reward charts (for younger children)
- Contract and token economies (for older children)
- Attributions
    - *Attributions about parents, parenting, children, childhood*
    - *How to handle jealousy*
    - *Budgeting time*
    - *Emotional challenges for children and foster carers.*
- Maintaining and generalising improvements
- Some additional strategies
    - *Assessing and formulating problems*
    - *Developing empathy*
    - *Role reversal*
    - *Conflict resolution and self-management*
- The course task

Session 5   Follow-up day
- Questions and queries
- Presentations: Course Tasks
- Problems encountered and solutions found
- Review of the programme.

Materials Each participant foster carer was provided with a Course Handbook. As indicated above, this was developed on the basis of a manual prepared by Herbert and Wookey (in press). This contained details of each of the sessions and information relevant to each. It was written and presented in what we hoped would be an easily accessible format. Participants were asked to read certain sections between sessions as part of their 'homework', and had an opportunity to discuss the material at the beginning of each session.

Homework One of the major tenets of learning theory is that people need to practice skills in order to develop them, and to receive feedback on their attempts to implement new skills and knowledge. Participants were therefore asked to practice some of the core skills between session, such as completing an 'ABC' chart, or keeping a record of the frequency or intensity of an aspect of a child's behaviour as a means of establishing a baseline which could be used to (i) better understand the behaviour and (ii) monitor progress.

Process The philosophy underpinning the training was organised to reflect a collaborative approach to problem-solving, such as that described by Webster-Stratton (1998) and Herbert and Webster-Stratton (1994). Foster carers are professional carers. Many are experienced parents, and all are doing a challenging job looking after children who are unable to live in their families of origin. Individually, carers often have considerable experience and expertise, and certainly in groups there is an abundance of both, providing a rich resource for all participants, including trainers. Effective training is training that succeeds in harnessing this expertise. This can only be done by recognising its presence, valuing it, and demonstrating that it is valued.

The training was designed to marry this expertise and experience with the specialist knowledge of the trainers and their experience of tackling child behaviour problems, albeit in different contexts e.g. residential care, working with families. The training was conceptualised as an opportunity for those involved to develop their problem-solving skills, in an applied way that would be relevant to participants. It contained a minimum of didactic presentation, and most of the programme involved using the carers' own experiences or situations as the means of learning about behavioural principles. In other words, it was rather 'Socratic' in nature. The trainers encouraged participants to reflect on their own knowledge and experience and used this to shape new knowledge and skills.

Trainers Two trainers ran the training programme: The first, Martin Herbert, was a clinical psychologist who has had a great deal of experience in working with troubled and troublesome children and young people. He took the lead role in the training. The other trainer was the grant holder. Geraldine Macdonald played a supportive role in the training. Both have written widely on the use of cognitive-behavioural approaches and have had substantial experience in running training groups. To minimise bias, all data were collected and analysed by a research associate recruited specifically to the project for this purpose, and who was not part of the training.

After each session the trainers met to discuss how the session had developed and to plan the next. These meetings addressed such concerns as: (1) keeping participants on task without seeming uncaring about non-training concerns, (2) sporadic attendance, and (3) non-completion of homework assignments. Decisions taken after discussing these concerns were applied in all the following week's training sessions.

Methodology

The Consortium of Directors who commissioned this project, via the Centre for Evidence-Based Social Services, were concerned to sponsor a rigorous study potentially capable of answering questions about the effectiveness of the training in question. One of the most secure ways of answering questions about the effectiveness of a particular intervention is by means of an experimental research design. The most common design is a randomised controlled experiment, in which research participants are randomly allocated either to receive the intervention or to a group that does not. All things being equal (e.g. no major problem in implementation) this approach to evaluation enables one to be confident that the outcomes are indeed attributable to the intervention, rather than some other factor such as changes in policy (see Campbell and Stanley 1973). This was the approach taken here.

Participants were randomly allocated either to a cognitive-behavioural training group or a waiting list control i.e. a group of carers who continued to receive usual services, and who were told that they would receive the training at a later date, should it prove effective. The Directors of the South West Consortium gave this undertaking.

Sample (Recruitment & Selection)

Sample Size.

The usefulness of power calculations is questionable for relatively small samples (Campbell and Stanley, ibid). Bearing this in mind, we estimated that in order to be able to identify statistically significant changes in children's behaviour we would probably need a sample size of 63 participants in each group[i]. In order to identify an impact on placement stability, we estimated that we would need a sample size of approximately 50 in each group.[14] Given the overall resource constraints of the study (both of money and time) a larger sample size was not possible. Our final sample size comprised 67 participants in the experimental group and 50 in the control group.

[i] See endnotes on page 88

[14] If we estimate that placement instability averages 30% and we take a 30% reduction as evidence of effectiveness, and if we assume a simple underlying probability distribution, then a sample size of 50 would give a 37% chance of detecting this effect at the 5% level (and a 95% chance of detecting it at the 10% level).

The participants.

The participants in this study were foster carers in six local authorities in the South West of England. At the outset of the project only three local authorities were involved, but due to the problems encountered in recruitment of foster carers to the study, this number was extended. Four of the local authorities in the study were unitary authorities. Two were large shire counties.

Although foster carers are not required to attend training as part of the requirement for maintaining their status as approved foster carers, the fostering teams at the participant departments recognised the need for specialised training in managing children's difficult behaviour, and indicated that a significant percentage of their foster carers had expressed a desire for such training.

Initial meetings were held between members of the research team and fostering officers to discuss the practicalities of the training, e.g. recruitment and training venues. The numbers of registered approved foster carers obtained from the first three participating local authorities were as follows:

- o   LA1: 89 (unitary authority)
- o   LA2: 82 (unitary authority)
- o   LA3: 76 (unitary authority)
- o   LA4: 316 (large shire county)
- o   LA5: 240 (large shire county)
- o   LA6: 170 (unitary authority)

For reasons of Data Protection we were not, in the first instance, able to approach foster carers directly. Instead, we provided letters and leaflets to the local authorities who forwarded these to foster carers, with a covering letter explaining their association with the project. We specifically asked that the information only go to foster carers engaged in short-term or long-term fostering i.e. to exclude respite foster carers or link workers.

The leaflet provided an outline of the aims of the project, what the training involved, who the trainers were, and dates of the training. It also stressed the strong evaluative element of the project and explained the random allocation of participants to training and/or wait-list control groups. Finally, it included guidelines of how foster carers who wished to do so could register their interest in participation. This was done directly to the research team, based at Bristol University, by filling a return slip attached to the leaflet and posting it in the stamped-addressed envelope provided. It was intended that registration for the study would close one month prior to the beginning of the training.

Attrition

Once we received indications of interest, we sent a questionnaire to foster carers asking for basic information, such as age, experience, how many years they had been fostering, and what age children they were approved to care for. Often, when this questionnaire was returned we discovered that the carers were fostering on a respite care basis, or were link workers. We therefore excluded such carers at this stage.

Table 4.1 provides an overview of the numbers of carers who expressed an interest in the project, those who agreed to take part, those who withdrew following randomisation (usually because they were allocated to the control group) and how they were allocated in terms of the six groups run. The Table is rather complicated. We have done our best to simplify the information, but the reality was complex. Some withdrew from the study once the dates and/or location of the training were confirmed[15]. Others withdrew once they realised they had been allocated to the control group. Even though this had been carefully explained, often in the context of meetings as well as via the written information, some carers were aggrieved at this outcome. We took this as an indication of the need for such training, and these disappointed carers, along with other control group carers frequently voiced this view.

[15] For example, finding a venue suitable for all foster carers in a large rural area such as LA4 was not easy. This is why some of LA4's foster carers were grouped with those in LA6 to form a training group for under 10s. Even then, some carers were unable to make the journey.

Figure 4.1: Recruitment and allocation of foster carers

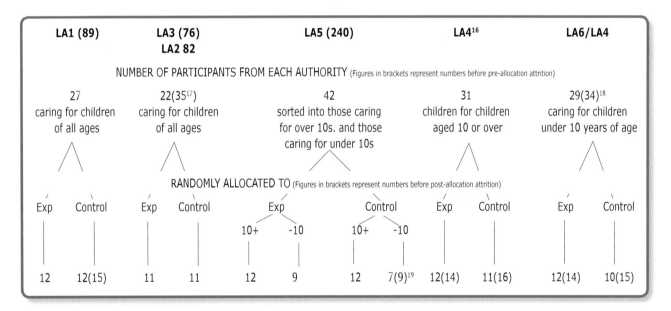

LA1 (89)	LA3 (76) LA2 82	LA5 (240)	LA4[16]	LA6/LA4
NUMBER OF PARTICIPANTS FROM EACH AUTHORITY (Figures in brackets represent numbers before pre-allocation attrition)				
27 caring for children of all ages	22(35[17]) caring for children of all ages	42 sorted into those caring for over 10s. and those caring for under 10s	31 children for children aged 10 or over	29(34)[18] caring for children under 10 years of age
RANDOMLY ALLOCATED TO (Figures in brackets represent numbers before post-allocation attrition)				
Exp / Control	Exp / Control	Exp 10+ / -10 / Control 10+ / -10	Exp / Control	Exp / Control
12 / 12(15)	11 / 11	12 / 9 / 12 / 7(9)[19]	12(14) / 11(16)	12(14) / 10(15)

[16] Excluding the area where the pilot group was run.

[17] We received 12 return slips from LA2, but 3 were from family link workers, 1 was a respite worker. We had asked that these carers NOT be invited to participate in the study.

[18] 20 of these were from LA6 and the remaining 14 were those who responded from LA4 and who looked after children aged 10 and under. Three of these carers subsequently dropped out because the venue was not convenient for them.

[19] We lost two carers after allocation from this control group.

Organisation of the groups

We had originally intended to run all groups according to whether or not carers were looking after children under- or over-ten years of age, and to run two groups within each of the three local authorities that had originally agreed to participate. This was to ensure that the case material and experiences of each participant were most likely to be seen as relevant to other members of the group. We soon ran into difficulties. First, it soon became clear that we were unlikely to recruit sufficient carers from one authority to run two groups. We were obliged to recruit two more local authorities. This enabled us to run one group in one authority (LA1) and a second drawing on carers from two adjacent authorities (LA2 & LA3). It was not possible, however, to constitute these groups as dealing with under- and over-tens respectively due to the small numbers of carers involved. In LA5 we were able to run two groups, one for carers looking after children ten years and under, and one for carers looking after older children. We ran one group in LA4 for carers looking after children over ten years, and in LA6 we ran a group for carers from LA6 & LA4 looking after children ten years or younger.

The implications of these very practical, time-consuming and frustrating obstacles are discussed in chapter 8 - Discussion.

Assignment

Because of the geographical distribution of foster carers it was not possible to make the allocation from the whole sample. Rather we were obliged to randomise within smaller geographical locations. Six training groups were run in total. Foster carers were randomly allocated from six clusters, using a random numbers table[20]. Table 4.1 (above) provides an overview of the process, from recruitment to allocation.

Measures used and data collected

The outcome measures used were:

1. A measure of participants' knowledge of behavioural principles as applied to children (O'Dell et al. 1979). Details of this instrument can be found in Appendix 1

2. The number of unplanned breakdown of placements. These data were obtained from interview data, which covered the month prior to the onset of training, the five weeks of training, and the six months after training

3. The Child Behavioural Checklist (Achenbach 1993)

4. A Foster Carer Satisfaction Questionnaire

Participants were interviewed before and after training, and at six months follow-up. Each interview schedule was developed specifically for the purpose of the study[21]. All interviews were tape-recorded after consent was obtained.

[20] The procedure described in Keppel, Saufley and Tokunaga (1992) was used. The Table A-1 provided in Appendix A of their book (p. 529) was used. The researcher entered the random number table "blindly", by having eyes closed and placing a finger somewhere on the page. He began reading a series of single-digit numbers in a left-to-right direction from this starting point. As the critical digits representing the coded treatments appeared in the table – 1 (training) through 2 (control) in this case – he recorded them on a sheet, which became the assignment sheet for the participants. This process was continued until all subjects had been listed in each condition.

[21] Interview Schedule 1 contained questions that were relevant to all foster carers, regardless of allocation to training vs. control condition. For Interview Schedules 2 and 3, questions had different degree of relevance depending on whether foster carers had participated in the training vs. control conditions: Interview Schedule 2 contained 4 questions, while Interview Schedule 3 contained 5 questions directly relevant to control participants.

The interviews were semi-structured and wide-ranging in scope. In addition to obtaining information on unplanned terminations of placements, the interviews were designed to enable us to contextualise the study, to better interpret the quantitative indicators, and to provide data of process variables.

Interview schedule 1[22]

The initial interview (pre-test) took about 90 minutes to complete. It was organised into six sections: *Section A:* Deciding to foster (6 items), *Section B:* Preparedness to foster (5 items), *Section C:* Effects on the family (3 items), *Section D:* Children fostered in the past (13 items including prior experiences of unplanned terminations of placement and the role played by children's behaviour problems in these), *Section E:* Children currently in their care (6 items) and *Section F:* The training programme (4 items covering motivation and expectations).

Interviews at the end of training (post-test) and at follow-up focused essentially on the training programme, how helpful participants had found it, and the extent to which they were using what they had learned.

Interview Schedule 2

The second (post-test) interview schedule took about 40 minutes to complete. It was divided into three sections: *Section A:* Current personal and social circumstances and programme evaluation (14 items), *Section B:* Knowledge at present (3 items), and *Section C:* Changes since attending the programme (7 items).

Carers who had participated in the training were also asked to complete a *Foster Carer Satisfaction Questionnaire.* This comprised 29 items covering a variety of different aspects of training and its impact. Carers were asked to rate each item on a scale of 1 – 7, e.g.

The major problem(s) that originally prompted me to participate in the training is (are) at this point:

Considerably worse	Worse	Slightly worse	The same	Slightly improved	Improved	Greatly improved

[22] Interview Schedule 1 contained questions that were relevant to all foster carers, regardless of allocation to training vs. control condition. For Interview Schedules 2 and 3, questions had different degree of relevance depending on whether foster carers had participated in the training vs. control conditions: Interview Schedule 2 contained 4 questions, while Interview Schedule 3 contained 5 questions directly relevant to control participants.

Interview Schedule 3

The final (follow-up) interview took about 30 minutes to complete. It was divided in 3 sections: *Section A*: Current personal and social circumstances (1 item), *Section B*: Knowledge at present (3 items), and *Section C*: Changes since attending the programme (10 items).

Carers who had participated in the training were also asked for their views on how training might be improved and what support structures they though were necessary to sustain any knowledge or skills they might have acquired as a result of training.

Procedure

All data were collected and analysed by a researcher acting independently. He was also responsible for the random allocation of participants to training vs. control conditions. When this was done, a letter was sent to relevant parties informing them of the outcome of the selection procedure. At the same time, the researcher contacted participants over the phone to arrange interviews. Those who were selected to participate in the training group were interviewed first, while the wait-list controls were interviewed shortly afterwards. All interviews were arranged at a convenient daytime hour, when children were at school. Interviews were tape-recorded, once consent was obtained. At the end of the interview, the *Knowledge of Behavioural Principles As Applied to Children (KBPAC)* was administered to foster carers selected for the training with instructions to fill it in and return it in a pre-paid envelope provided, before the start of the training. A 2-week period was allowed for those in the wait-list condition.

During interviews, foster carers selected to participate in the training were asked not to disclose the content of the training with others until the end of the training programme. Such an action was necessary to safeguard the evaluative element of the project, considering that all foster carers, in addition to regular home visits by social workers and fostering officers, attend monthly group meetings, organised by their fostering teams, to discuss issues pertaining to fostering. Of course, we do not know to what extent carers complied with our request. As indicated earlier, foster carers in the wait-list condition were informed from the onset that the same training would be available to them, once evaluation of the programme has been completed.

A few days after the end of the training programme, the researcher contacted foster carers to arrange interviews. As before, those in the training condition were interviewed first, while foster carers in the wait-list control condition were interviewed afterwards. The *Knowledge of Behavioural*

Principles As Applied to Children (KBPAC) was administered to all foster carers again after the end of the interviews.

This process was repeated six months after the end of training. All foster carers were told that they would be kept informed about the outcome of the study, once data collection had been completed. Foster carers in the waiting-list control condition were told that they would be kept informed about the next training opportunity from their respective fostering team.

Chapter five

Results

In this chapter we present the results of those data analyses pertinent to the six hypotheses we set out to test. Each one is listed, together with a summary of the results. Detail of the analyses underpinning these results is then presented. It is possible to read the chapter without reading these more technical paragraphs, each headed 'Analysis'. We begin by discussing some of the steps we took to ensure that the conclusions we drew were reliable.

Deciding when something was statistically significant

A statistical level of .05 was chosen for the analyses of all outcome measures. In other words, we deemed it statistically significant if the data suggested that there was no more than a 5% probability that differences between the two groups (training/experimental and no-training/control) had arisen due to factors other than membership of that group, or were due to chance. Statistical significance does not guarantee meaningful results i.e. results that would make practitioners or policy makers want to change their practice, but it is an important indicator of whether or not the intervention in question might be having an impact on those who are receiving it.

SPSS (version 10.1.0) was used for all the analyses that follow.

General considerations

The first step in the data analysis was to explore the data collected to get an idea of any patterns within it. It was important to see whether the data met the criteria necessary for the statistical procedures we intend to use, that is to decide whether to use a parametric or a nonparametric procedure[23] (see Field 2000). With the exception of scores on the KBPAC scale all data collected are qualitative (categorical). For these variables, non-parametric tests were used as a means of testing the hypothesis of interest.

---

[23] According to Gibbons (1993) parametric procedure should be used when both of the following are true: 1. The data are collected and analysed using an interval or ratio scale of measurement. 2. All of the assumptions required for the validity of that parametric procedure can be verified. Otherwise, a nonparametric procedure should be used. This means that a nonparametric procedure is appropriate when any of the following is true:
1. The data are counts and frequencies of different types of outcomes.
2. The data are measured on a nominal scale.
3. The data are measured on a ordinal scale.
4. The assumptions required for the validity of the corresponding parametric procedure are not met or cannot be verified.
5. The shape of the distribution from which the sample is drawn is unknown.
6. The sample size is small.
7. The measurements are imprecise.
8. There are outliers and/or extreme values in the data, making the median more representative than the mean.

Preliminary analysis and final sample

A preliminary analysis indicated no significant effects and/or interaction of the Local Authority variable with any other variables. Since no significant effect of this variable was observed, this factor was excluded from all subsequent analyses.

One hundred and seventeen participants comprised the final sample, of which all but two were white. Of these, 67 foster carers (female foster carers=52, male foster carers=6, couple foster carers=9) participated in the training group and 50 in the control group (female foster carers=37, male foster carers=6, couple foster carers=7). The ages of these participants ranged from 32 to 65 years, with a mean age of 45 years. Experience of fostering (in years) ranged from one to fifty years, with a mode of one year (i.e. carers with one year's experience occurred more frequently than carers with other profiles). The overall mean was 8.68 years.

Tests for equivalence between groups at pre-test

The purpose of randomisation is to ensure equivalence between those in the intervention group and those in the control group. When the sample size is small, as in this study, imbalances in the groups can occur despite randomisation. This is exacerbated when, for example, participants drop out of the study. For these reasons we undertook some statistical tests to explore whether or not at the outset of the study the groups were equivalent in factors that might otherwise influence the outcomes we were examining. We examined the carers' knowledge of behavioural principles, their fostering experience, their experience in dealing with behaviour problems, and the number of children they fostered.

Knowledge of behavioral principles

Although relatively low, the level of attrition that occurred during the training raised concerns over the initial equivalence of the two groups. We therefore compared the groups' baseline knowledge of behavioural principles, as indicated by their scores on the KBPAC. This showed the groups to be comparable.

Analysis: A t-test[24] designed to discern significant differences between groups was conducted on the mean scores obtained by both groups before training (pre-test). The comparison with respect to KBPAC scores (training group $\underline{M}$=19.08 vs. control group $\underline{M}$=17.83) produced a t-value of −0.87 (df=103, p=.39), which was not statistically significant at the .05 level.

Fostering Experience

Since experience has been found to be positively related to placement stability (Boyd & Remy 1978), participants in the two group conditions were compared with respect to this variable. No statistically significant differences emerged.

Analysis: The Mann-Whitney U statistical test was used for testing differences between groups on the years of fostering

[24] Independent t test.

experience at pre-test. The test works by looking at differences in the ranked positions of scores in the different groups. Table 5.1 presents the results of the analysis.

Table 5.1. Summary of Mann-Whitney test results on fostering experience

	Group Mean Ranks			
Scale	Training (67)	Control (50)	U statistic	p
Fostering Experience (years)	62.46	54.36	1443.00	.20

Experience in dealing with a range of behavioural problems

Although the two groups did not differ significantly in terms of years of fostering experience, we were concerned to ascertain if they differed with regard to the range of behavioural problems they had encountered. Any differences between the groups in terms of their experience in handling a range of behaviour problems might account for any differences that emerged in their abilities to manage these.

The groups differed only in relation to their experience of dealing with children engaged in offending and self-harming behaviour. Carers in the control group reported greater incidence of having encountered the behaviours in question than participants in the training condition.

Analysis: Chi Square and Fisher's Exact Test were calculated for data relating to carers' experience in dealing with 25 behaviour problems.

Number of children fostered

Because foster children moved into and out of the participants' homes during the course of the study, an analysis of the data pertaining to the number of children cared for was performed. This was done in order to assess the initial equivalence of the two groups with respect to that variable and the maintenance of that equivalence over time. Table 5.2 presents the number of children fostered across the three time periods for participants in the training vs. control group. The results show that there were significant differences across time with regard to the number of children fostered by participants in the training group. These participants increased the numbers of children they fostered from before training (Time 1) to the end of training (Time 2), and again from the end of training to six months follow-up (Time 3). No statistically significant increases occurred for participants in the control group. Whilst not formulated as an outcome measure, this was an interesting difference and one we explore in chapter 8.

Further, comparisons *between* training vs. control group at each of the three time periods showed no statistically significant differences between the two groups in the number of children fostered at each time point.

Analyses: The Friedman test (nonparametric equivalent of a one-sample repeated measures design) was used to analyse whether there was any significant difference in the number of children fostered across time for carers in both groups. Table 5.2 presents the number of children fostered across time periods for training vs. control group and the results of the two analyses.

Table 5.2. Number of children fostered across time period for training vs. control groups

Group	Time 1	Time 2	Time 3	Friedman Test
Training (n=46)	85	88	97	$X^2=7.64$, df=2, p=.02
Control (n=40)	69	70	79	$X^2=.76$, df=2, p=.68

The results of the analysis for the training group suggest that there were significant differences across time with respect to the number of children they fostered ($X^2=7.64$, df=2, p=.02)[25].Visual inspection of the data in Table 5.3 shows that for participants in the training group there was a slight increase in the number of children fostered from Time 1 to Time 2 and a further increase from Time 2 to Time 3.

The analysis on the number of children fostered by the control group did not reveal any statistically significant results ($X^2=.76$, df=2, p=.68). For participants in the control condition the number of foster children from Time 1 to Time 2 remained almost the same, while a slight increase was noted from Time 2 to Time 3.

Comparisons between the number of children fostered by carers in the training group vs. those in the control group were made using the Mann-Whitney test. The results of the three between-groups comparisons are presented in Table 5.3. None of the comparisons was shown to be significant, indicating that there were no significant differences in the number of fostered children between training vs. control groups at the different time periods.

Table 5.3. Between-group comparisons relating to number of fostered children at different time periods

Comparison	Mann-Whitney U	P*
Time 1: training vs. control	855.00	0.56 (>1)
Time 2: training vs. control	846.00	0.49 (>1)
Time 3: training vs. control	856.50	0.57 (>1)

*p values should be multiplied by three (the Bonferroni correction) to allow for the multiple comparisons (cf. Altman, 1997). Adjusted p values are included in parentheses.

[25] The annotation as suggested by Altman (1997) is used here: X^2 is used to denote the test statistic while x^2 is used to refer to the theoretical distribution.

Hypothesis 1

Participants in the training programme condition will score significantly higher on the KBPAC scale than foster carers in the wait-list control condition.

This proved to be the case. Over time, foster carers in both groups improved their scores on the *Knowledge of Behavioural Principles Applied to Children (KBPAC)* scale, but only for the training group did the increase reach statistical significance. At Time 1 (pre-training baseline) the differences in the mean KBPAC scores between the two groups was not significant, as should be the case. At each subsequent time point, however, participants in the control group scored significantly lower than those in the training group (as measured by mean scores).

Analyses: Mean scores on the KBPAC scale were analysed using a 2 (group) x 2 (time) mixed-model analysis of variance (ANOVA), with time as a within participants factor. Table 5.4 summarises the results of the analysis, while Table 5.5 presents the mean scores. Analysis of the significant interaction revealed the following:

Table 5.4. Repeated measures analysis of variance of scores on the KBPAC scale[a]

Source of variance	df	MS	F	p
Group	1	533.72	5.61	.020
Group Error Term	84	95.13		
Time	1	552.02	47.55	.0001
Group x Time	1	165.61	14.26	.0001
Group x Time Error Term	84	11.61		

[a] **Number of participants:** Training = 48, Control = 38

Table 5.5. Means of KBPAC scores

Group	Time 1	Time 2	Row means
Training	19.23	24.81	22.02
SD	(7.97)	(7.30)	
Control	17.66	19.29	18.47
SD	(6.47)	(7.21)	
Column means	18.44	22.05	

The significant main effect for group ($\underline{F}(1, 84)=5.61$, $p<.02$) indicates that, regardless of time period, participants in the control condition ($\underline{M}=18.47$) scored significantly lower than participants in the training condition ($\underline{M}= 22.02$). Further, the analysis revealed a significant effect of time ($\underline{F}(1, 84)=47.55$, $p<.0001$) and a significant group x time interaction ($\underline{F}(1, 84)=14.26$, $p<.0001$). The significant main effect for time showed that participants, regardless of training vs. control group condition, scored significantly higher at Time 2 (Time 1 $\underline{M}$=18.44 vs. Time 2 $\underline{M}$=22.05). Analysis of the significant time x group interaction revealed results in the expected direction.

A simple main effects analysis using the within participant error term (MS=11.61) revealed a significant increase in the mean KBPAC scores over time for participants in the training condition (Time 1 $\underline{M}$=19.23 to Time 2 $\underline{M}$=24.81). For participants in the control group, the analysis, using the same error term, showed no statistically significant differences in mean KBPAC scores (Time 1 $\underline{M}$=17.66 vs. Time 2 $\underline{M}$=19.29).

A simple main effects analysis using the pooled within error term plus the between error term[26] (MS= 52.68) showed the following: At Time 1, as should be the case, mean scores on the KBPAC scale between training ($\underline{M}$=19.23) and control ($\underline{M}$=17.66) participants were not found to be significantly different. As expected, analysis of mean KBPAC scores between training vs. control participants at Time 2 was found to be significant (training $\underline{M}$=24.81 vs. control $\underline{M}$=19.29).

Hypothesis 2

Participants in the training programme would be significantly more likely than foster carers in the wait-list control group to use behavioural techniques in managing children's behaviour.

The range of behavioural techniques/strategies foster carers employed in dealing with difficult behaviour(s) was analysed for participants in the training vs. control conditions for the three time periods. As can be observed from Table 5.6, participants in the two conditions did not differ significantly with respect to the range of behavioural techniques they employed at Time 1.

[26] As recommended by Kirk (1982) and Keppel, Saufley & Tokunaga (1992).

Table 5.6. Results of Chi Square and Fisher's Exact Test (FET)[27] for behavioural strategies used by foster carers at Time 1 (pre-training).

Behavioural strategies employed	df	x^2	FET	p
1 Dependent on young person's age	1	.04		.83
2 Dependent on young person's personality	1	.52		.47
3 Dependent on situation/behaviour	1	1.37		.24
4 Positive reinforcement (tangible) [28]	1	2.86		.09
5 Praise / social reinforcement		.46		
6 Tokens			.69	
7 Negative reinforcement				
8 Differential reinforcement[29]	1	.00		.98
9 Grounding	1	.00		.98
10 Time out[30]	1	.03		.86
11 Response Cost[31]	1	.33		.56
12 Contracts			.31	
13 Principles of good discipline/rule setting[32]	1	.65		.42
14 Consistency (e.g. united front)	1	.69		.41
15 ABC Analysis[33]	1	1.35		.25
16 Clear communication[34]	1	2.17		.14
17 Plan ahead/diversion[35]	1	2.11		.15
18 Knee-jerk reaction (e.g. shout back)			.07	
19 Calling on a third party				
20 Other (least behavioural) [36]	1	4.67		.03*
21 Good child care[37]	1	.00		.98

[27] A test for independence in a 2 x 2 table. It is most useful when the total sample size and the expected values are small (cf. Altman, 1997).

[28] e.g., rewards.

[29] e.g., praise good things, ignore bad.

[30] e.g., walk away, put in their room.

[31] e.g., take away privileges.

[32] e.g., firm but fair, boundaries, non-judgemental, non-blaming, sometimes challenge, not react-be calm, become quieter when shouted at, carry through punishments.

[33] e.g., relate to problems, sit and observe patterns, sit and reflect on situation, look for reason, step back-then step in.

[34] communicate understanding, listening, be assertive, , honest, straight-forward.

[35] think ahead of them, avoid confrontation, bring humour into it, diffuse situation, remove child from situation.

[36] e.g., deal with things as they come along.

[37] make them feel important, provide reassurance and security, bed-time story.

After training (post-test)

At the end of the training there was evidence that training had a significant effect on whether or not carers made use of tokens, grounding, and the ABC analysis. For tokens, the significant result indicates that there is an association between training and whether participants indicated they had used this strategy or not. What an association means is that the pattern of responses (i.e. the proportion of participants who cited the strategy to the proportion that did not) in the two group conditions is significantly different. In this case none of the participants in the control condition indicated they had used tokens, whereas 10% of those in the training did. Perhaps related to this, 16% of those in the control condition indicated the use of grounding compared with only 4% of those in the treatment group. Grounding is a rather blunt instrument compared with strategies such as response cost, and the training encouraged carers to take a more strategic and measured approach to infringements of rules etc. This is somewhat speculative, however.

With regard to the use of ABC analyses, only 9% of participants in the control condition indicated they had used such a strategy compared with 42% in the training group. This way of thinking about behaviour is now common currency, to some extent, but participants in the training group had spent a lot of time practising the skills associated with the careful analysis of behaviour, and examining its usefulness with regard to the problems they were dealing with. Throughout the training many carers commented on the fact that the ABC analysis had encouraged them to step back from a situation, observe what was going on and try to think strategically about how best to handle something. Others observed that this helped them to stay calm and in control of what had hitherto been very taxing situations.

For the remainder of the strategies covered in the training programme, there were no significant differences between the two groups at the end of training.

Analyses: Table 5.7 shows that the results of the analysis regarding behavioural strategies employed at post-training (Time 2), revealed significant results for tokens, grounding and ABC analysis. For tokens and grounding strategies, the Fisher's Exact Test is significant (p<.05) indicating that participation in the training programme had a significant effect on whether participants used the technique in question. For the use of the ABC analysis of behaviour, the chi-square is highly significant (p<.0001).

Table 5.7. Results of Chi Square and Fisher's Exact Test (FET) for behavioural strategies used by foster carers at Time 2 (post-training)

Behavioural strategies employed	df	x^2	FET	p
1 Dependent on young person's age			.73	
2 Dependent on young person's personality				
3 Dependent on situation/behaviour	1	4.50		.03
4 Positive reinforcement (tangible)	1	.38		.54
5 Praise / social reinforcement		.22		
6 Tokens			.04*	
7 Negative reinforcement			.58	
8 Differential reinforcement			.32	
9 Grounding			.04*	
10 Time out	1	1.69		.19
11 Response Cost	1	1.22		.27
12 Contracts			.58	
13 Principles of good discipline/rule setting	1	.22		.64
14 Consistency (e.g. united front)	1	2.71		.10
15 ABC Analysis	1	13.19	.0001*	
16 Clear communication	1	3.44		.06
17 Plan ahead/diversion	1	.53		.47
18 Knee-jerk reaction (e.g. shout back)			.55	
19 Calling on a third party			.42	
20 Other (least behavioural)			.23	
21 Good child care				.06

At the six months follow-up, the use of the ABC by carers who had participated in the training group remained statistically significant compared with those in the control group (see Table 5.8). The only other behavioural strategy reported statistically more often by one group than the other was the use of response cost. 37% of control participants cited using the strategy compared with only 18% in the training group. This result is not in the direction expected i.e. we would have expected those in the training group to make more use of such an explicitly behavioural strategy, and indeed we had anticipated that carers in the training group would report more use of a wider range of behavioural strategies than was the case. Possible explanations for this are discussed in the next section.

Analysis: Results of the statistical analysis relating to behavioural strategies employed at follow-up are presented in Table 5.8. For response cost, the significant chi-square indicates that the group condition had a significant effect on whether the strategy was cited as used. For the ABC analysis of behaviour, the chi-square reached the same level of high significance as at post-training. For tables 5.6 – 5.8 * indicates significant at the .05 level.

Table 5.8. Results of Chi Square and Fisher's Exact Test (FET) for behavioural strategies used by foster carers at Time 3 (6-month follow-up)

Behavioural strategies employed	df	x^2	FET	p
1 Dependent on young person's age			.24	
2 Dependent on young person's personality			.24	
3 Dependent on situation/behaviour			.33	
4 Positive reinforcement (tangible)	1	3.00		.08
5 Praise / social reinforcement		.29		
6 Tokens			.29	
7 Negative reinforcement			.46	
8 Differential reinforcement			.46	
9 Grounding			.26	
10 Time out	1	2.14		.14
11 Response Cost	1	3.84		.05*
12 Contracts			.15	
13 Principles of good discipline/rule setting	1	.04		.84
14 Consistency (e.g. united front)	1	1.75		.19
15 ABC Analysis	1	14.98		.0001*
16 Clear communication	1	1.48		.22
17 Plan ahead/diversion	1	2.31		.13
18 Knee-jerk reaction (e.g. shout back)			.56	
19 Calling on a third party			.13	
20 Other (least behavioural)			.54	
21 Good child care			.07	

Hypothesis 3

For children in the experimental group there would be fewer unplanned terminations of placements in which behaviour problems were implicated.

This proved not to be the case. In fact, carers in the training group showed a slight increase in the number of unplanned terminations of placement from post-training to follow up. Over the same period those in the control group reported a slight decrease in unplanned terminations of placement in which behaviour problems were implicated. These data are difficult to interpret. In the event, the sample of foster carers involved in this study had a below-average rate of unplanned terminations of placement where behaviour problems were deemed by the carers to be a significant factor. The vast majority of those who participated in the training said that they had seen improvements in their child's behaviour (*Foster Carer's Satisfaction Questionnaire*), and that the training had contributed to this improvement. These are only self-report data, and we have no comparable data from those in the control group. We discuss data pertaining to validated measures of children's behaviour change below.

Analyses: Visual inspection of the data pertaining to the number of unplanned placement breakdowns for group conditions and time periods, presented in Table 5.9, shows that for the training group there was a very slight increase in the number of unplanned terminations from post-training (Time 2) to follow-up (Time 3). For the control group, there was a very slight decrease in the reported number of unplanned terminations between post-training (Time 2) and 6-month follow-up (Time 3).

Table 5.9. Number of unplanned placement breakdowns across time periods for training vs. control groups.

Group	Time 2	Time 3
Training	2 (n=55)	4 (n=49)
Control	5 (n=45)	4 (n=40)

Further, comparisons between training vs. control groups across the two time periods were made. The results of the two between-groups comparisons using the Mann-Whitney test are presented in Table 5.10. It shows that differences in the number of unplanned placement terminations both at Time 2 and Time 3 between training and control groups were not found significant.

Table 5.10. Between-group
comparisons for the number of
unplanned placement breakdowns
at different time periods.

Comparison	Mann-Whitney U	P
Time 2: training vs. control	1145.00	0.15 n.s.[38]
Time 3: training vs. control	962.50	0.76 n.s.

Calculating the number of placement breakdowns in this way can appear as a rather inexact comparison. This is because some of the carers compared had a number of foster children over the period of the study, while others had only one or even none. The months at risk was therefore calculated for carers in the training and control conditions: and analysed using a 2 (group) x 3 (time) mixed-model analysis of variance (ANOVA), with time as a within participants factor.

No significant difference between the two groups was found at the .05 level, $F(1, 84)=1.99$, n.s. The non-significant main effect for group shows that, regardless of time period, participants did not differ on their months at risk scores (training $M=52.34$ vs. control $M=35.86$). Further, the analysis revealed a significant effect of time, $F(2, 168)=25.92$, $p<.0001$. The significant main effect for time showed that participants, regardless of training vs. control group condition, had greater months at risk at Time 3. No other results were significant.

Table 5.11. Months at risk across
time period for training vs. control
groups (Standard Deviations in
parentheses)

Group	Time 1	Time 2	Time 3
Training (n= 46)	49.26 (63.98)	48.89 (60.85)	58.87 (64.54)
Control (n=40)	34.45 (40.77)	32.78 (40.92)	40.35 (44.39)

Results of analyses conducted between training vs. control group *across* the three time periods are reported in Table 5.12 below. None of the results were significant.

Table 5.12

Comparison	One-way analysis of variance	P*
Time 1: training vs. control	F(1,116)=1.16	.28
Time 2: training vs. control	F(1,99)=2.32	.13
Time 3: training vs. control	F(1, 85)=2.33	.13

* exact p values.

NOTE: The analysis does not take into account that some carers have had more difficult children than others.

[38] Non significant.

Hypothesis 4

Participants in the training programme would report a significant reduction in the range of problems that they found particularly difficult or challenging, compared with foster carers in the wait-list control.

This did not prove to be the case. At each time point we asked participants what they found particularly difficult or challenging, and coded their responses. On the basis of the number of responses each participant reported, we calculated an index representing the proportion of reported difficult behaviours by summing the number of behaviours reported as difficult and challenging by each participant and dividing the number by 25 (total number of behaviours that could be listed). Although the number of reported problems significantly reduced over time, this was the case for both groups. There were no differences between the two groups at any time point.

Analyses: The Friedman test (nonparametric equivalent of a one-sample repeated measures design) was used to analyse whether there was any significant decrease (or reduction) in the proportion of reported difficult behaviours across time for carers in both groups. Table 5.13 presents the proportion of behaviours reported as difficult and/or challenging across the three time periods for participants in the training vs. control group and the results of the two analyses.

As expected, the results of the analysis for the training group suggest that there was a significant decrease over time with respect to the proportion of reported difficult behaviours (X^2=21.69, df=2, p=.0001)[39]. Visual inspection of the data in Table 5.13 shows that for participants in the training group there was a reduction in the proportion of reported difficult behaviours from Time 1 to Time 2 and a further decrease from Time 2 to Time 3.

Disappointingly, and contrary to expectations, the analysis on the proportion of perceived difficult behaviours for the control group also revealed statistically significant results (X^2=9.56, df=2, p=.008). For participants in the control condition the proportion of perceived difficult behaviours from Time 1 to Time 2 also decreased in a similar pattern to the one observed in the training group, while a further slight (and similar) decrease was noted from Time 2 to Time 3.

Table 5.13. Proportion of perceived difficult behaviours across time periods for training vs. control groups

Group	Time 1	Time 2	Time 3	Friedman Test
Training (n=67)	.07	.07	.05	X^2=21.69, df=2, p=.0001
Control (n-50)	.08	.07	.05	X^2=9.56, df=2, p=.008

[39] The annotation as suggested by Altman (1997) is used here: X^2 is used to denote the test statistic while x^2 is used to refer to the theoretical distribution.

Further, comparisons between training vs. control group across the three time periods were made with regard to the proportion of *perceived* difficult behaviours. The results of the three between-groups comparisons using the Mann-Whitney test are presented in Table 5.14. None of the comparisons was shown to be significant, indicating that there were no significant differences in the proportion of perceived difficult behaviours between training vs. control groups at the different time periods.

Table 5.14. Between-group comparisons relating to proportion of perceived difficult behaviours at different time periods.

Comparison	Mann-Whitney U	P*
Time 1: training vs. control	1620.00	0.75 (>1)
Time 2: training vs. control	1672.00	0.99 (>1)
Time 3: training vs. control	1593.50	0.64 (>1)

* p values should be multiplied by three (the Bonferroni correction) to allow for the multiple comparisons (cf. Altman 1997). All adjusted p values (included in parentheses) are greater than 1.

Hypothesis 5

Foster carers in the training programme would report success in dealing with behaviour problems.

We hoped that not only would foster carers be more likely to use cognitive-behavioural methods, but that they would do so successfully. We looked to two sources of data on this. First, we used the Child Behaviour Checklist to ascertain the overall extent to which children's behaviour improved (Achenbach 1993). This is a commonly used and psychometrically robust measure of child behaviour problems, covering children aged 4-16. It has versions for carers, teachers and self-report for older children. Whilst there are distinct advantages in collecting data from a range of sources, we were only able to collect information from carers.

At the outset of the study, all study participants (in both training and control group conditions) were asked to fill in a behavioural checklist (Achenbach 1993) relating to a young person whose behaviour they found difficult and challenging. If they were caring for more than one child we asked them to choose the child they were most concerned about. This was done for two reasons: i) to gather information regarding the severity of behaviour problems study participants were dealing with, and ii) to establish a baseline for subsequent comparisons.

The same behaviour checklist was again distributed at the time of the 6-month follow-up interview to those carers who still had the same young person placed with them. Due to movements of foster children in and out of foster carers' homes, we obtained matched behavioural checklists for a total sample of 46 children. Twenty were looked-after by participants in the control condition and 26 were looked-after by participants in the training condition.

Secondly, we asked foster carers to undertake at least one piece of work aimed at using behavioural strategies to effect behaviour change, and to produce a summary of this work. We discuss these 'course tasks' as these projects were called, in the next chapter. Here we report the findings from the analysis of changes in Child Behaviour Checklist scores from before the training to six months follow up.

The Child Behaviour Checklist Scores

Initially, data were entered and scored using the cross-informant program for the CBCL/4-18, version 5.3 (Achenbach 1997).

Syndrome Scales

The program displays eight syndrome scales derived from analyses of checklists filled out by parents or teachers of children referred for mental health services, or by referred youths. These syndrome scales have been given descriptive labels based on the items empirically found to make up each syndrome and are called Withdrawn, Somatic Complaints, Anxious/Depressed, Social Problems, Thought Problems, Attention Problems, Delinquent Behaviour, and Aggressive Behaviour. Second-order factor analysis has shown that the Withdrawn, Somatic Complaints, and Anxious/Depressed scales form one broad-band group, while the Delinquent and Aggressive Behaviour scales form a second. These groups have been labelled Internalising and Externalising respectively.

Total Problem Scores

The program also displays scores for the total number of problem items scored as present, the Total Problem Score, and Internalising and Externalising scores. Additionally, T scores comparing these last three sums to the normative samples of non-referred children are presented. The main function of the T scores is to facilitate comparisons of the degree of deviance indicated by children's standing on different scales and instruments. Based on percentiles for the normative sample, the T scores provide a convenient way of quickly judging whether a parent reports relatively many or few competencies and problems, as compared to parents of non-referred children. Achenbach (1991) suggests that statistical analyses using the T scores for the Internalising, Externalising, and Total Problem scores would yield results similar to those using the raw scores (scores given by the carers). Statistical analyses pertaining to these three sets of scores are presented next.

Analyses

Tests of normality (Field 2001) indicated that scores in the three scales are normally distributed. As a result, parametric statistics were used in their analysis. Mean scores obtained were analysed using a 2 (group) x 2 (time) mixed-model analysis of variance (ANOVA), with time as a within participants factor.

Internalising Scores

Internalising scores reflect the degree to which children exhibit feelings of anxiety and depression, somatic complaints, and withdrawal.   The results of the statistical analysis relating to mean Internalising scores did not reveal any statistical significant results.

Table 5.15 presents mean Internalising scores between control vs. training group conditions at Time 1 (pre-training) and at Time 3 (follow-up). Visual inspection of the means show that the foster children's Internalising scores between training and control groups remained the same from pre-training to follow-up.

Table 5.15. Means of Internalising scores

Group	Time 1	Time 3
Training	65.31	64.23
SD	(11.15)	(10.89)
Control	64.40	64.70
SD	(13.19)	(13.48)

Externalising Scores

Externalising scores reflect the degree to which children's behaviour reflects delinquent and aggressive behaviour.   As with Internalising scores, the results of the statistical analysis relating to mean Externalising scores did not reveal any statistical significant results.

Table 5.16 presents mean Externalising scores between control vs. training group conditions at Time 1 (pre-training) and at Time 3 (follow-up). Visual inspection of the means show that the foster children's Internalising scores between training and control groups remained the same from pre-training to follow-up.

Table 5.16. Means of Externalising scores

Group	Time 1	Time 3
Training	64.46	62.81
SD	(11.36)	(11.52)
Control	63.40	63.55
SD	(14.10)	(15.28)

Total Scores

The results of the statistical analysis relating to mean Total scores did not reveal any statistical significant results. Children with carers who had undergone the training showed no more improvement in their overall scores than children whose carers were in the control group.

Table 5.17 presents mean Total scores between control vs. training group conditions at Time 1 (pre-training) and at Time 3 (follow-up). Visual inspection of the means show that the foster children's total scores between training and control groups remained the same from pre-training to follow-up.

Table 5.17. Means of Total scores

Group	Time 1	Time 3
Training	58.04	58.58
SD	(13.05)	(12.67)
Control	58.40	58.80
SD	(14.11)	(13.64)

Whilst data from foster carers should be viewed as only one component of comprehensive assessment, it is clearly an important source of information. We collected data from training group foster carers on the use they made of what they had learned on the course, in relation to one or two specific problem behaviours that they targeted for change. These data are not discussed here, as there are no comparable data from the control group, and not all foster carers completed this task. Instead, we present these findings in the next chapter. They suggest that some of those who completed the course were able to analyse situations, select, and implement behavioural interventions with some success. It may be that the CBCL change scores reflect as much the magnitude of the problems that these looked-after children have, than the carers effectiveness at bringing about change, and that it would be unreasonable to expect those problems to respond markedly simply to short-term improvements in management strategies. We discuss this issue in the penultimate chapter of the report.

Hypothesis 6

Foster carers would feel more confident in their abilities to manage difficult behaviour.

The qualitative data we collected in the course of this study provide ample evidence to support this hypothesis. Carers generally said that the course had made them more confident to deal with difficult situations and difficult behaviour.

Carers most frequently pointed to the fact that the course had encouraged them to take two steps back from a situation and to think about what was going on *before* intervening. By the end of training the concept and importance of undertaking a functional analysis (an 'ABC' analysis) was well ingrained in participants' ways of thinking. This enabled them to deal with situations more calmly and this was thought to benefit both the carers (who were less stressed by events) and the children (who experienced more thoughtful and considered responses from carers who were less emotionally aroused).

They reported that undertaking an ABC analysis sometimes highlighted their role in maintaining problem behaviour, as well as other factors influencing it, some of which were outside their control. The following quotations are all taken from the follow-up interviews conducted six months after the carers had completed training.

Nothing to learn Some foster carers, albeit the minority, felt that they had gained little from the training. Thus, in response to the question 'to what extent have you been able to apply any of what you've learnt in the training programme' some respondents said:

> 'We did not learn anything more that we already knew"….I think because we've been fostering for 11 years and so we didn't learn anything out of it because we've been there, we've done that, we probably could have taught them what they could have done …Everybody said that; that they were learning more from us than they were learning from them. He (trainer) was talking to the wrong people, he was giving all this wealth of information he had that didn't need to know all that; they (participants) need to know different things. We thought we would turn up and be given strategies to deal with certain situations. If you are confronted by so and so, this is what you do, or this is what we recommend you do. And the reason you don't do this is because…'

Carer 02

This respondent was one of a carer couple who attended one of the earlier groups. The trainers had said from the outset that the course was not a 'quick fix' course, but a programme designed to help carers think analytically and strategically about the nature of the problems they were dealing with, and to develop a range of interventions that they could deploy in appropriate situations and appropriately tailored. These carers made it clear on several occasions that they were looking to be told how to handle physically violent older children, and to that extent there was a mismatch from the start. The impact on this group was also very negative, with other carers complaining that they dominated the group and were preventing them from contributing and/or learning. Notably, these carers were amongst those who did not complete the Course Task and did not attend the follow-up session.

Something to learn

Others were more positive and indeed enthusiastic. In response to the same question, two other foster carers who had participated in the same training group as the ones above, responded:

'It's more subtle than we thought, isn't it? We were at one time, we were saying that we hadn't gained much from it because it wasn't different.... It was geared more towards younger children and 14 years old with all these problems. I think.....As you go on, you realise you are drawing on it; all these little bits that's got in there that haven't been, what you call, the main process of the programme, because it was mainly directed towards younger children, but there's been other aspects of the programme that wasn't in direct relation to what they were discussing, but they've been useful in bringing to handle the situation. That's weird! I cannot break it down.

But the actual programme itself was useful in giving you hints. There weren't exactly structured procedures to give. Because in the programme there were exact procedures to give small children in individual cases, but we found out that there were things that we spoke about then are relevant; that you can use in another situations with the sexually problemed children and that....

In a way, although the structure was not what we appreciated, not structured exactly to our needs, there was still facts in that programme that we've been able to draw on for some strange reason.'

Carer 07

Lots to learn

The majority of carers were extremely positive about the training programme. Here is a sample of quotations from those who were most positive, responding again to the same question:

'I find myself automatically thinking o.k., what did we do half an hour ago that could have started this off, and if it's something I can pinpoint, I could then start to talk or say, well, that happened, is this what caused it and I can usually work out an answer for dealing with it then depending on what the cause was'.

Carer 64

'It's (referring to the training programme) something new; it took a while to get going, but once we started, I stuck to it and it really worked!'.

Carer 100

A similar response was given by other foster carers:

'First I would work hard, but it's becoming easier the more I've used them' (referring to the strategies taught during the training). 'I would enjoy more training along the same lines. I don't think the course was long enough'.

'I think we should always be open to learn, be open to new ideas/suggestions'.

Carer 78

'Before I did the training programme I was quite ready for her (foster child) to go, but now I try to ignore some of the little things and deal with the bigger problems. I now feel more in control and have a better relationship with her now'.

Carer 76

'Because I've never seen this behaviour this child was displaying, especially the self-harming, I needed support, because my husband was away a lot then as well. And I really needed someone to talk to me at the other end of the phone and not make me feel stupid. But when we went to the course everything makes sense; and I talked to him (trainer) about lots of little things that she did and he made sense of that and then I could look at it when she was doing it and understand it. So if you've got the support and people help you understand the behaviour you can then work on that behaviour instead of thinking: ' Well, go to your auntie P. Well, I can remember just like getting a neighbour come in and just walking out and going for a drive in the car because I was so wound up and I know if I'd stay here, I'd have hurt her, which is not in my personality'.

Carer 24

'The training was an eye-opener because it made you sit and think, it made you think about situations as opposed to getting frustrated over situations. You step back and think: 'right, why are they're doing this? They are doing this because of this'.

Carer 45

Increased confidence was probably the most significant finding from this study. Whilst we did not observe the kinds of changes we had hoped to identify with regard to children's behaviour or, indeed, to carers' abilities to 'think and talk behaviourally' with regard to behaviour *management*, there is evidence to suggest that this might point to the need for a longer programme which provides more opportunities to develop intervention skills. We return to this issue in Chapter 8.

Chapter six

Foster carers' use of behavioural methods

We asked all those who participated in the training to undertake a piece of work, referred to as the course task. The material given to carers is included as Appendix 2. The purpose of the task was to get some indication of the extent to which foster carers had understood the material covered in the course, their abilities to analyse behaviour using social learning theory, and their effectiveness in choosing and implementing cognitive-behavioural strategies. We are not able to use this material to examine whether or not carers who have received the training are more effective than those who have not, because of the absence of comparative data. The material available to us does, however, give us some important information about the effectiveness of the course and suggests ways in which it might be strengthened in the future.

What was asked?

Carers were asked to choose a child in their care about whom they were concerned, to describe the problem in behavioural terms, and say how serious they considered it. They were then asked to identify what they saw as the 'triggers' for behaviour and the 'pay-off' or consequences. They were then asked to undertake an ABC analysis, and on the basis of that, together with other information they had about the child, to decide what an appropriate intervention would be. In order to monitor progress carers were asked to record the frequency of behaviour before and during their intervention (or any other, appropriate measure).

How many carers completed the task?

The first observation to make is that not all carers undertook or completed this piece of work. For some carers this was because they did not have children placed with them at the time they participated in training or subsequently. Others were caring for children on a respite basis, and these children rarely presented behaviour problems. In some cases, however, carers reported difficulty in finding the time to do this. Insofar as the course was designed to encourage carers to use the skills they learned, this represents an element of failure. Thirty-one carers submitted course tasks. Some submitted more than one, and some submitted tasks they conducted as couples (three couples).

Did the course tasks provide evidence that carers could analyse behaviour using social learning theory?

The course tasks demonstrate that most foster carers had a working knowledge of how behaviour is influenced by its antecedents and consequences, and were able to analyse particular pieces of behaviour within the ABC framework. In keeping with this, carers were most adept at identifying (or hypothesising) what factors might trigger behaviour (antecedents) and what the 'pay-off' (reinforcement) might be for particular patterns of behaviour. These were generally 'proximal' antecedents i.e. things in the immediate circumstances, but some carers were aware of the impact of 'distal' antecedents i.e. factors in the child's more distant past or early learning history. Carer 2 provides one example:

> **Carer 2** tackled a problem of a child who crammed food into his/her mouth at meal-times, and when offered sweets etc. The carer completed an ABC analysis that highlighted the fact that when the carer was watching the child slowed down but as soon as eye contact was lost the cramming recommenced. The carer did not identify any particular 'pay-offs' and hypothesised that the behaviour may have been a consequences of early experiences e.g. neglect.

Were carers able to set clear goals?

Generally, carers were able to set themselves clear goals. Here are some goals:

> 'Not to get out of bed immediately T wakes'.

> 'We would like P's eating habits to improve so that P could be taken out to eat e.g. McDonald's'.

> 'Play by self, or make friends of ... own age and do more age-related activities. Allow J at times to play by self. To move away from the situation when it gets difficult or asked to do so'.

> 'Express ... feelings so that I can understand the root cause of R's anger. When I try to separate R from the person receiving the burnt of R's anger, to do what I ask'.

Clearly, there is some scope for further operationalising these e.g. being specific about what 'improved eating habits' might look like for P, rather than another child; 'age-related activities'. Carers could, in fact, generally do this if prompted. The fact that this aspect of cognitive-behavioural 'thinking and doing'– together with some others – was not as well ingrained as we had hoped, suggests that a short training programme is insufficient to embed changes in thinking and acting, some of which are quite fundamental. Our considered view is that the length of training, exacerbated by the size of the groups, is probably a major reason why the training appeared to be less effective than we had hoped.

Were carers able to choose appropriate interventions?

Carers appeared quite adept at choosing appropriate strategies. Some carers opted to record the work they had done with regard to a problem they had discussed in the groups. To this extent, then, they were implementing strategies that the group had settled on. Nonetheless, the strategies often represented a fundamental change in the way that the carer had been attempting to deal with the problem, or had been reacting to it. Here are three examples, beginning with an intervention that did not bring about the desired effects:

> **Carer 6** wanted to stop one of the children she was caring for (E, aged 12) from giving contrary instructions to other children in the family. This was high frequency behaviour with serious potential consequences for other children. In general, the carer thought the child was trying to parent the others (perhaps as a result of previous experiences) and it appeared to be worse on days when E was stressed. The 'pay-off' identified was that 'other children are told off for not following instructions and their confusion amuses E. The child gains attention through being in trouble and is given an excuse to lose their temper or cry'. This situation was discussed in the group and the carer decided to speak to E and to say that whilst she valued E's help it was confusing the children if both gave them instructions and that she would let E know if she needed E's help. She planned to use a points system and to gradually fade the number of times she asked E to help/give instructions to the others. **Results**: the behaviour got worse. The carer observes that E started out well but that the other children 'got increasingly angry as E's attitude changed'. More importantly, other behaviours began to emerge which made his instruction giving trivial.' The frequency chart completed by the carer confirms a lessening of the problem followed by a general increase.

> **Carer 13** was concerned about F, aged 15. She wanted to be able to 'talk things through calmly from the outset, and stop the arguments before they get worse'. She chose to state clearly to F that she did not want a heated argument, and left the room saying that she would not argue, but

would discuss issues later. This was designed to make space for F (and the carer) to calm down. The carer was careful to make time to discuss things later. **Results**: the intervention was deemed to be 'quite successful': 'after a few times of being consistent and keeping calm it seemed to work.' The frequency chart supported the carer's view of success.

Carer 13 also wanted to improve the communication skills of C, aged 13. If the carer asked C a question C would 'stay silent until pressed/encouraged … often still makes non-productive noises or gestures … shrugs/grunts/grins, …. (says) simply 'OK' '. The triggers appeared to be difficult questions or personal questions (e.g. about siblings, parents). The 'pay-off' was thought to be not taking responsibility or having to face up to problems. The interventions chosen by the carer were: 'encouragement and praise; grandma's rule (When…then….), consistency and never to make a promise that the carer couldn't keep'. **Results**: 'quite successful'. The carer reported 'reasonable responses, but hard work to extract a response most of the time'. The carer felt guilty about being insistent and consistent.

For the most part carers did not label interventions in behavioural terms, and when they did (as with Grandma's rule above) they did not always do so correctly. Grandma's rule (or 'Premack's principle') was clearly used appropriately in the above example. It is essentially a 'when, then' rule. It is not an 'if, then' rule, but some carers found difficulty in separating these two ideas. Sometimes – though relatively rarely – they indicated a more fundamental misunderstanding, as with this carer who refers to 'bribery' rather than reinforcement:

Carer 19 sought to tackle G's outbursts of temper that resulted in quite serious aggression towards other people. G was 11 years old. G's behaviour appeared to be triggered when in a crowd, with other children without adult supervision, or generally when under pressure e.g. thinks someone is picking or pushing G. The 'pay-off' appears to be that G thinks s/he is hurting those hurting G. The carer reports that the strategy deployed was to stop the physical contact right away and divert G's attention to other things, including TV, toys, talking, sweets etc. The carer described the latter as 'bribery' indicating some misunderstanding of certain aspects of cognitive-behavioural strategies.

Results: The carer reports the intervention was 'quite successful', defined as G's outbursts having become a little less aggressive.

There was evidence in the course task material of very carefully planned interventions, such as those deployed in the following examples:

Carer 7 was concerned about one of her foster children, K aged 8 years, who was argumentative and when playing with other children could easily hurt them e.g. kicking, twisting arms and hitting. She thought one of the most common triggers for K's behaviour was following a meeting with social workers, or when let down at the last moment with regard to a planned contact arrangement. That said, she described the behaviour as 'constant'. She thought the 'pay-off' for K was relief from stress, and that when in an argumentative situation K feels more secure and in control. Carer 7's goals were for K to 'keep up friendships with other children, to understand how s/he feels and what makes K angry so that s/he can learn control'. She also wanted K to feel confident. These goals were not as specific as one would hope, but the intervention chosen was a weekly star chart to be used between the home and the school. The carer also sought to ignore as much behaviour as possible, using diversion and intervening in a way she thought would break the cycle. For example, she said that she would 'ignore and bring in other topics. If child still argues after 20 minutes with no help from myself, bring hand down on table very hard and shout 'no more'.' **Results:** The carer reports that these strategies were 'quite successful' and that K is now able to tell them when she/he hurts children, to make eye contact, and is generally more relaxed, going a couple of days without being argumentative. She observes that visits from agency staff and contact arrangements are outside their control.

Carer 20 focused on stopping the children she was caring for (ages 10, 8 and 6) from arguing whenever they got into the car. Their arguments were about where each was going to sit. She opted for a reward and response cost system whereby for each time they got into the car without arguing they could earn one penny extra to the twenty pence they received each week to spend on penny sweets. When they argued, twenty pence would be deducted. She wrote 'I kept saying I would use this method, but didn't get round to it. However, when they saw me take a pen and paper in to the car they knew I meant it and things improved considerably. Now I rarely get more than the odd comment which they quickly tell me wasn't a complaint! Found they started agreeing seating arrangements before they got into the car.

In response to the question 'What were the main problems you encountered' the last carer wrote 'Getting round to doing it.' This was not an unusual piece of feedback from carers who, like parents, are often juggling a range of priorities. Knowing that it will help is often not sufficient to ensure that something is adopted – that seems to depend on someone reaching a point when the costs of not doing so start to outweigh the costs that are certainly involved in implementing a behavioural strategy.

How well were carers able to monitor behaviour and behaviour change?

Carers were able to report improvements in a child's behaviour (or deterioration or no change). They were not generally adept at using the frequency charts, however. There was evidence of difficulties in this area during the training, and with hindsight the trainers thought that they should have given more attention to this, and to ensuring that participants fully grasped the principles underpinning the interventions that were covered in the programme. Similarly, the 'squeeze' on time meant that there was less behaviour rehearsal within the groups than the trainers would otherwise have wished. That is to say, most of the work on interventions was based on short presentations and discussion, albeit around issues that the carers themselves brought to the groups. A fundamental principle of learning theory is that talking and listening are not very effective as a means of bringing about behavioural change. The implications are: (i) that the groups should perhaps have been smaller and/or, (ii) the training programme should be longer, in order to ensure that sessions contain a sufficient 'practice' component. Again, we discuss this in more detail later.

Were carers effective in their use of cognitive-behavioural methods?

It is not possible to give a categorical answer to this question. Here is why. First, these carers were looking after extremely difficult children, whose behaviour problems were often triggered (and maintained) by factors outside their control. Even when they knew the antecedents for their child's challenging behaviour, and had a good idea about what was maintaining it, they were not always able to intervene. Here are three examples. All carers report some success, and are clearly aware of how the distal antecedents influencing each child's behaviour make behaviour change a long and demanding process, for both carer and child:

Carer 3 focused on the 'defiance' of an eleven-year-old child who had been with her for some time. This defiance was particularly problematic in situations in which the child was behaving inappropriately and the carer wished to calm him/her and get him/her to behave more appropriately e.g. not hitting out at others when she/he is checked. The carer thought the most common triggers for the behaviour were tiredness, problems outside the foster home brought about by contact with absent family members, and an inability to express her/her emotions in words. The child was developmentally delayed. The 'pay-off' identified by the carer was 'somebody else feeling (R's) pain'. She thought that if she could help the child to express his / her feelings then R's defiance and aggression might lessen. This carer chose first to concentrate on her own reactions, learning 'to remain calm, softly spoken and in control. 'If I feel myself losing control I leave R until I am calm and then begin again.' Her other intervention was to remove R from the company (or the company from R) and to supervise R's playtime at intervals throughout the day, changing activities when necessary. **Results**: 'In the last four months the behaviour is much more controllable. For the most part I know before the behaviour is manifest when the danger times are. I have learnt that by leaving R for a short time and then talking to R, although R rarely talks to me, I can return R to a more willing state'. The carer has learned that at the present time R is not able to express emotions, and she makes careful allowance for this. She is also aware that this leaves her having to second guess the root causes. She writes 'I am always aware that I could have it wrong, but just talking seems to help'.

Carer 4 was concerned about a 13 year old child in her care who did not want to wash/brush teeth, change clothes etc. The distal antecedents were identified as having been put in a bath of hot water and burnt. The carer says it has taken seven years for this child to go into the shower and she still needs to coax a lot. Sometimes however, no amount of coaxing will work. The carer writes: 'There are no particular triggers for S, just bad memories... so the slow, long, long, long, encouragement and mountains of patience is the most important.' The carer has tried a range of strategies including patience, encouragement, and talking about why personal hygiene is important. She describes that in the past she has become upset and resorted to banning S's computer/TV etc. but has learned that this is not the answer. **Results:** The carer reported some success, but no details were given. No ABC analysis was provided and the goals were not particularly specific i.e. to improve self-esteem and to encourage S to take care of him/herself better. The carer wrote 'I have had to learn to be patient and step back – no point in trying to reason with S when S is angry, S just gets angrier and can be quite upsetting.'

Carer 2 was tackling the problem of a child who crammed food into his/her mouth at mealtimes, and when offered sweets etc. (see above). The strategy used was one suggested in the group; that of putting his/her spoon down between every one or two mouthfuls. **Results:** The carer reports some success, but also observes 'P's problems have arisen since he/she has started to have contact with his/her parents'.

Secondly, some carers had to cope with frankly unreasonable demands. Even the most skilled and experienced behavioural practitioners would find it difficult to implement behaviour change in some circumstances, particularly without support from others. Here is one example:

Carer 11 was concerned about the refusal of 8-year-old, H, to go to school. She described the behaviour as 'not going to school saying I am not going, I am not getting in taxi, not putting shoes on, lots of swearing, sitting down folding arms, crying, screaming, shouting, slamming doors, hurting the two other children in household, smacking, kicking, spitting, hair-pulling, pushing, hitting out at adults, throwing things, kicking chair, doors.' This single carer was responsible for *three* quite difficult children. The trigger was the approach of the time to go to school (or clubs) and the taxi arriving. The 'pay-off' was thought to be having to go in a separate taxi, with the carer, and sometimes staying home with her/him instead of going to other activities. The carer introduced a short-time reward chart with daily tuck shop which the child could 'buy from' at the end of each day using his reward stickers. Whilst she reports a little success with some improvement, the carer found that H was not concerned about these rewards.

The frequency and stress of the behaviour were given as reasons why this carer was unable to complete a behavioural record (frequency chart). In the group we were very concerned at what this carer was being expected to cope with, on her own. Trying to change the behaviour of one child is challenging enough, but to cope with three is probably more than one should reasonably ask of a single foster carer. However – the carer adds: 'One of my children said s/he was ready to work on his/her bed-time wetting. We booked an appointment with nurse just as I started this course. Because of information on this course about bed-wetting, and the best way to work with it being the bell and pad, I was better equipped to work with this. So in fact the child went from wetting every night to - by the time the course had ended and the children had moved on from me – s/he was only wetting one night a week.'

Finally, carers did not always provide sufficient evidence to support their claims of behavioural improvement, particularly when this was modest. This was, we think, because of their lack of understanding with regard to the frequency charts. Although used to recording for social services, they were unused to keeping the kinds of records that support single-case evaluations. Here are two examples of carers who report some success, but who provide no observational data or other corroborating evidence:

Carer 9 focused on S, aged 3, who screamed and argued when she/he could not have her/his own way e.g. chocolate before lunch. Not unusually for a child of this age, S's behaviour was triggered by not getting what she/he asked for. This often happened in the company of other children or parents, and the carer thought the 'pay-off' for S was being taken home and receiving her undivided attention. The carer's goal was to be able to hold a conversation with another parent without S constantly seeking attention, and not screaming when she/he did not get her/his own way. The carer's strategies comprised diversion (occupying the child with an activity) and explaining, for example, that she/he cannot eat chocolate before lunch, but could take it home and eat it afterwards. **Results:** The carer reports that the strategies were 'quite successful'.

Carer 1 was experiencing problems with a young child, T, who was waking early and disrupting the entire family. T was also being affected in terms of ability to concentrate at school, so tired that T can't keep awake beyond 7.00 pm. And so on. The carer easily identified the 'pay-off' for this early waking (attention from all sorts of people and – she hypothesised – a sense of being in control, and could attribute the origins of the problem to night terrors that she/he had had when placed). The carer reported trying the use of star charts (with mixed or partial success) and then response cost which was much more effective. The carer labelled this strategy simply as 'punishment' but it was in keeping with what we had discussed about using effective (strategic rather than 'blanket') sanctions i.e. if you wake up early and disturb your sibling then you will go to bed ten minutes earlier. **Results:** The carer's report concludes: 'T has maintained his/her efforts to stay in bed longer in the mornings, looks less tired as a result, and my husband and I feel less pressurised as we were listening out every morning for over 12 months for the first sign of T awakening, trying hard so that the rest of the household were not disturbed'. Unfortunately, the carer has now to unlearn the habit of early waking herself.

Of the 31 problem behaviours targeted by carers, respondents reported that in nine cases their intervention was very successful in bringing about improvements in behaviour. In a further nineteen cases, the intervention was classed as 'quite successful', having brought about some improvement in the problem behaviour, and in the remaining three cases, data were missing on two, and in the last one the behaviour deteriorated. The graphs provided by two of the carers who classified their work as 'quite successful' demonstrates considerable improvement over a three-week period. Here are examples of some of the instances where carers report considerable success:

Carer 18 produced two course tasks. The first concerned a 10 year old, N, who used bad language and took no responsibility for anything, always saying 'Not my fault'. The most common triggers for this behaviour were thought to be the presence of others e.g. if the other child in the family brought a friend around. Other triggers included bedtime, mealtimes etc. The carer thought that the pay-off was that these responses made N feel in control of situations. N also seemed to enjoy getting other people into trouble. At school the situation was sufficiently serious for the teachers to be considering removal. The carer introduced a number of interventions, including: very clear and firm boundaries, a points system both at home and school, and what they saw as grandma's rule ('if you don't argue this evening you can go on the computer for one hour'); praise for points earned on the points system, and logical consequences 'if you can be nice to the people who live in the house, you can have a friend to tea'). **Results**: the carer describes the outcome as 'very successful' and the accompanying frequency chart supports this. The carer says N now knows boundaries and rewards. They still have to tackle problems with smearing, sulking and rudeness, but clearly feel they are making progress using similar strategies. 'Now quiet, a happy (child), better at school'.

Carer 3 also sought to reduce arguments between the two siblings she cared for, aged 10 and 11. Her goals were 'to teach the two children to occupy themselves, talk to each other i.e. how to solve their problems by sharing time on an object, borrowing and paying back, and the skills needed to meet each other half way.' Her strategies were careful monitoring of their activities at weekends, when they were much in each other's company, 'teaching them to do things separately, talking about the benefits of sharing and putting time-limits on activities like computers so that equal time could be spent by each child'. **Results:** the carer writes 'I had completed this exercise by the time the children had returned to school after the Christmas holidays. 7th January. It is now the end of January and the children's behaviour has improved amazingly. It has even carried over to places like Youth Club and School. The children are separating into individuals with different likes and dislikes and have found the confidence to do what they want to do alone. We still have the occasional squabble but I am now aware of 'danger times' like missed contacts, or visits from professionals where their past life is the topic of conversation. Consequently I feel in control of the situation and can therefore manage the behaviour more effectively.'

One of the carers (Carer 8) who reported 'no change', had said very early on the group that she thought that 'nature' rather than 'nurture' was the predominant influence on children's behaviour. Further, she thought there was nothing one could do to change 'hard wired' patterns of behaviour. She did not attend all sessions, but those that were attended clearly failed to influence her thinking. She appears to have absorbed relatively little of what was being covered.

> **Carer 8** looks after a 17-year-old, M. M tells lies. The goal was clear enough – not to tell lies, but this is a difficult goal to measure. The carer was unable to identify either triggers or consequences, and did not complete an ABC analysis. She/he tried the following punishments 'No TV, Read books. Not allowed out to play'. Perhaps not surprisingly the carer reports that the behaviour did not change. S/he thought this would not happen 'until he/she was allowed to spend as he/she wants and go where he/she wants.'

The other carers who reported 'no change' in the problems they tackled were a couple who were trying to find a way of stopping D, the 13-year-old in their care from breaking his/her spectacles. D wanted contact lenses. In the preceding 6 months D had broken four pairs of spectacles, and had had repeated repairs done between times. Because of D's age the carers were reluctant for D to have contact lenses. They tried not responding too negatively, as this was one of the 'pay-offs' for D, and tried to work with the optician to persuade D of the unsuitability of lenses for young people under 16. Eventually they removed the glasses when they were not being used for reading or watching TV. The time between breakages improved but they reported that D grasped every opportunity to damage them. The carer who reported that the behaviour she tackled had deteriorated, catalogued a series of events in the child's life (e.g. bereavement) that comprised plausible explanations. For reasons of preserving anonymity these details are not reported here.

We conclude this section with some examples of success, as perceived by the carers.

> **Carer 10** looked after a 10-year-old child, L, who told lies, shouted, screamed and behaved 'in a way that is immature' e.g. says 'its not me, no I didn't'. The triggers identified by the carer were: peers making fun of L, L not understanding something, L feeling threatened or uneasy with a situation. The 'pay-off' was thought to be that L gets out of things by behaving in this way and gets attention, even if it's negative. The carer adopted three strategies. The first was talking quietly and in shorter sentences. The second was explaining (quietly) why lying is counter-productive. The

third was to ignore really trivial things and to start praising the smallest things (differential reinforcement). **Results**: talking quietly and explaining things was very successful in making an impact, and that differential reinforcement was 'quite successful'. This carer produced a frequency chart that indicated that the lying decreased, but that it was not a high frequency behaviour to begin with. It was the significance of the behaviour for the family, rather than the frequency, that made it so serious.

Carer 12 chose to tackle two problems presented by J, aged 9 years. She wanted J to listen to instructions (e.g. laying the table) and then to carry them out within a reasonable time, and to do up her/his shoes properly i.e. tie uplaces tightly. The carer saw the child's history as the historical (distal) trigger. J had been shouted at and had rude signs made at him/her. Current triggers were the availability of others to tie J's laces. J also observes that it is 'cool' not to have one's laces done up. The 'pay-off', in her opinion, was that everyone else gets cross, J doesn't have to do what s/he has been asked to do, and gets a lot of attention. The intervention decided upon by this carer was response cost – to take time off J's TV programme(s) and to stop J going to youth group as J falls over playing games if the laces are not done up properly. **Results**: this approach succeeded in improving J's behaviour in terms of complying with most instructions i.e. doing things promptly. It was not successful in terms of tying shoelaces or laying the table (the latter was identified as a particular problem for the family as it delayed meals). The carer also learned that at school others tied J's shoes i.e. intermittent reinforcement. This carer provided a frequency chart of the number of times J was slow in getting ready for school. The chart shows some improvement, albeit from a low baseline.

Carer 17 looked after A, aged 11. The carer was concerned about homework disputes with A. She said A 'argues, lies, is secretive, destructive, swears, convinces me any which way that (s/he) hasn't any homework'. The trigger for such encounters was homework times. The 'pay-off' is that when A convinces the carer that there is no homework to be done, A gets to play. The carer introduced 'Grandma's rule ('if you do this, then you can go out etc.') and consequences ('logical consequences') – the carer said that after doing the ABC 'I took an interest in the homework, used homework diary, asked questions and gave a *little* assistance when necessary, but let A face the consequences from A's teacher for poor or no homework e.g. detention or double homework). Made own decisions on what A preferred by being given the choice'. **Results:** the carer describes the outcome of this intervention as 'very successful'. She writes: the child's relationship with us improved (remained undamaged) and A eventually took responsibility for doing (his/her) own homework – achieving 'A' and 'B's. Thank you for introducing us (me) to an effective method for managing difficult behaviour.' The frequency chart reflects the carer's report.

Contextualising behaviour

What is not immediately evident from the above records, or from the quantitative data reported earlier, is the trouble carers (and trainers) took to understand 'why' behaviour was occurring, after looking at 'what' was happening. We were at pains to help carers critically reflect on how a particular intervention or response might be experienced by an individual child, given his or her history, and to try to tailor interventions accordingly. This often entailed structuring interventions that would enable a child to open up about his or her feelings (e.g. asking him or her to write a letter) or reassuring them about their place in the home. The training programme also looked at other important factors such as how foster carers handle situations in which they do not find particular children easy to like, or if things are going badly for them personally e.g. they have relationships problems, or the foster child's behaviour is impacting adversely on their own children. All of these issues are crucial elements in developing an effective behavioural approach, but the research evidence suggests that they do not provide an alternative set of techniques for influencing behaviour. The emphasis in this report is therefore on the experience of carers in implementing behavioural interventions, albeit interventions chosen and implemented in the light of these other important factors.

Practical problems

Carers experienced a range of practical problems in trying to implement these approaches. These included time (which for some carers was a more constrained resource than for others), having to deal with more than one child, lacking support from other institutions such as school or the child's social worker, and having their endeavours thwarted by relatives of the child or – for older children – the child's peers. In some instances it was possible to make constructive suggestions about how best to tackle these, but for others there was little that carers could do. These difficulties reflect life, and the difficulties they present for carers seeking to deploy cognitive-behavioural approaches are not unique. There is nothing in these day-to-day challenges that make cognitive-behavioural approaches less likely to succeed than others, and carers are at least well informed about the limits of their likely influence, and where they could seek to extend in some circumstances e.g. some carers liased effectively with teachers.

Generalising behaviour

One section of the training programmes focused particularly on ways of planning for the generalisation and maintenance of behaviour change, although this issue came up throughout the programme.

Chapter seven

Foster carer satisfaction

Each session of the training was evaluated via a brief, session-specific questionnaire distributed and collected by the trainers. These questionnaires asked participants to provide a numerical score in response to the following questions, with '1' indicating 'very poor' and '5' indicating 'very good':

o   How well was the session organised?

o   How well was the programme material presented?

o   Were the topics covered in sufficient depth?

o   How well were the practice issues explained?

o   How well did you feel supported by the others in the group?

o   How well do you feel your opinion/contribution was valued?

o   To what extent do you feel you are making progress at this stage of the course?

In general, feedback was very positive, but of course this feedback was going directly to the trainers.   Although participants were told they did not need to put their names on the forms, most did, and so the feedback was not anonymous. These data were used primarily for the purpose of helping the trainers to plan subsequent sessions or groups.

In order to elicit a more robust picture of participants' views of the training, they were asked to complete a longer questionnaire, the *Foster Carer Satisfaction Questionnaire*. This was completed anonymously, and sent directly to the researcher responsible for data collection and data analysis. A total of 48 questionnaires were received. Some respondents occasionally missed a question.

In one of the groups there were two participants (a couple) who were particularly difficult to engage, and who had a rather adverse effect on the functioning of the group as a whole (as perceived both by the trainers and by other group members). In the following summary of responses to the *Foster Carer Satisfaction Questionnaire,* these two respondents account for the negative 'tail' (never more than three participants).

Satisfaction with the Programme

All but seven of the respondents said they were either satisfied (25) or very satisfied (16) with the training they had received. Most respondents reported improvements in the behaviour problems that had prompted them to participate in training (see Figures 7.1 and 7.2). The majority of carers thought that their child's behaviour had improved in general since participating in the course, and most were satisfied with the degree of progress:

Figure 7.1 Satisfaction with the programme

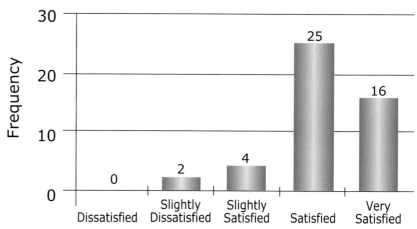

Figure 7.2 Improvements in problems that promoted participation in the course

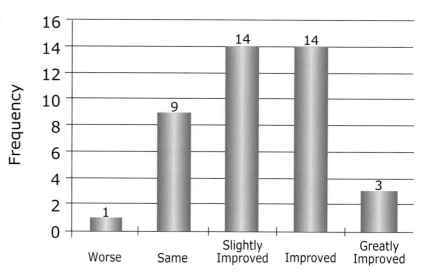

All but nine foster carers saw the training programme as having helped bring about these changes (11 thought it had 'helped slightly', 15 that it had 'helped', and 13 that it had 'helped very much'). 71% of carers were either 'optimistic' or 'very optimistic' about the prospect of a satisfactory outcome for their foster child's behaviour. Just over 7% said they were either 'confident' or 'very confident' in their ability to manage behavioural problems by themselves, both now and in the future. Overall, over 82% indicated that they felt very positively about the future, and all but five said they would 'recommend' (n=20) or 'strongly recommend' (n=23) the programme to other carers.

The teaching format We asked carers to say how difficult they had found the range of teaching methods used. Carers were asked to circle one of seven descriptors from 'extremely easy' through to 'extremely difficult'. Table 7.1: summarises the data. The majority expressed the view that the verbal information given by the trainers was 'easy' or 'extremely easy', as was their demonstration of skills. 'Practice of skills with trainer' received a more mixed response. This was perhaps because this was less pronounced an aspect of the course than was intended, or would have been the case had the groups been smaller (and/or the training longer). This lack of emphasis probably exacerbated the challenges presented to participants by requests to practice things at home. In addition to other pressures on their time, any lack of confidence would reduce the chances of homework being completed. Practice within the sessions would have increased confidence.

Table 7.1: Views on the level of difficulty presented by various teaching methods.

Teaching format	Extremely easy	Easy	Somewhat easy	Neutral	Somewhat difficult	Difficult	Extremely difficult
	%	%	%	%	%	%	%
Verbal information	15	63	8	8	6	0	0
Skills demonstration	11	67	9	9	4	0	0
Practice of skills with trainers	11	49	21	8	11	0	0
Practice of skills at home	0	31	31	15	21	2	0
Home work assignments	2	21	25	10	35	4	2
Written materials	10	42	29	13	5	0	0

Perceived usefulness of types of training

Having ascertained carers' views on the easiness or otherwise of particular training methods we asked them to say you useful they found each of them. Table 7.2 summarises their responses:

Table 7.2: Perceived usefulness of teaching and learning methods

Teaching format	Not useful in the extreme	Not useful	Somewhat not useful	Neutral	Somewhat useful	Useful	Extremely useful
	%	%	%	%	%	%	%
Verbal information	0	0	0	4	10	33	52
Skills demonstration	0	0	2	4	21	43	30
Practice of skills with trainers	0	0	0	13	10	50	27
Practice of skills at home	0	0	0	13	26	45	17
Home work assignments	0	0	2	19	15	56	8
Written materials	0	0	0	8	4	58	29

With regard to carers' perceptions, we conclude that the trainers succeeded in developing an accessible handbook, and in presenting information in ways that carers found easy to understand. The area that presented most difficulty for carers was putting skills into practice between sessions, and carrying out homework tasks. Most recognised these aspects of the training as both important and useful. The difficulties they encountered ranged from unexpected events e.g. a crisis with the child, the placement of another child, through pressures of time, to – for one or two carers – an unwillingness to co-operate with this aspect of the training.

Perception of the trainers

Participants were generally very pleased with the teaching they received. The lead trainer, Martin Herbert, was known to some of the carers from his appearances on television programmes. His reputation and status (as a clinical psychologist), and his clinical knowledge and skills (including his group work skills) were a major factor in the participants' satisfaction with the training. All but two of the participants rated the trainers' teaching as 'high' or 'superior' in quality. 87% thought the preparation undertaken by the trainers for each session was also 'high' (72%) or 'superior' (15%). 91% of carers said they were either 'very satisfied' (48%) or 'satisfied' (44%) with the interest and concern shown by the trainers for their problems, and all but three said they thought them 'helpful' (28%) or 'extremely helpful' (66%). The remaining three respondents said either that they were neutral (n=1) or saw the trainers as only 'slightly helpful'. With the exception of one person who remained neutral, those who answered a question about how much they liked the trainers said they 'liked them' or 'liked them very much' (45% and 53% respectively).

Chapter eight

Discussion

Only two of the five hypotheses that were formulated were clearly proven. These were the hypotheses that said that participants in the training group would score significantly higher in terms of their knowledge of behavioural principles as applied to children, compared to their colleagues in the control group, and report increased confidence in their ability to deal with difficult behaviour. This last relied only on qualitative data pertaining to the training group, based as it was on questioning about the impact of the training. One other hypothesis received partial support. This was the hypothesis that foster carers in the training programme would report success in dealing with behaviour problems. We assessed this by looking at the progress of particular children in each foster home, measured by the Child Behaviour Checklist (Achenbach 1993), and also by analysing information provided by those foster carers who had participated in the training and who were asked to report on a behavioural project. Only the last provided evidence that carers were able to analyse behaviour and implement behaviour change strategies with some success. Unfortunately, only half of those foster carers who were asked to completed this work, and there is no comparable data from the control group, i.e. we do not know if they too could analyse children's behaviour and intervene appropriately, or with what results. There were no differences detected between the two groups in relation to their use of behavioural strategies (coded by the independent assessor), in relation to unplanned terminations of placements in which behaviour problems were implicated, or in the number and/or range of behaviour problems that carers found particularly difficult or challenging. What then, should we conclude?

We should be rightly suspicious of attempts to explain away results, but it is also negligent to disregard lessons learned and plausible explanations for why a particular pattern of results have fallen as they have. This is one of the first randomised controlled trials to be run in UK social services for a considerable time and there are important lessons to be learned about the technical and logistical challenges of mounting rigorous evaluations of this kind. There are also implications for less rigorous methods of evaluation. We wish to raise a number of points in this chapter, and to draw out some of the implications as we see them, for practice, policy and research. They fall under three major headings: limitations of the training programme, broader contextual factors and lessons for evaluation research.

Limitations of the training programme

This was an expensive evaluation compared with many other projects. The cost was just under £200k, including the cost of training itself. Most funders will not fund both an evaluation and the programme being evaluated (although it is not unusual for some government departments to set aside some money to evaluate new programmes in which it is investing substantial sums of money). This project was, therefore, in a particularly privileged position to be able both to fund an intervention and evaluate it. That said, the budget was small in respect of doing both. In order to ensure that funds were available for independent data collection and analysis – essential, given that one of the researchers was participant in the training – the training programme had, to some extent, to be tailored to the budget. In the first instance this was not something we were too concerned about. As we looked to the broader parent-training literature, and previous experience of such programmes, the programme we developed looked as if it would be sufficient to achieve satisfactory outcomes. We provided an accessible and fairly detailed handbook, which we thought would act as a useful back-up and resource for carers to consult between sessions, and we had planned weekly homework tasks to ensure that carers practiced new skills in the environment that mattered most – home. Our experience of running six groups suggests that there is ample scope for improving the programme. Some of the issues have been alluded to in earlier chapters, but in summary, they are as follows:

1. The programme achieved its aims in relation to teaching carers the importance of understanding *what* is going on, and *when* and *where* behaviour occurs – the ABC of behavioural interventions. Carers learned to hold back from the 'why' question and return to it only when they had a firm grasp of the observable aspects of problem behaviour. They were less adept at identifying behavioural interventions and the course tasks suggest that these were, in fact, less well understood than we had hoped. Thinking of the balance of activities within the groups as they unfolded (as opposed to the formal programme), this is probably understandable. Much of the time was spent trying to make sense of children's

behaviour, and less time was spent on planning and implementing behavioural change strategies.

2. Carers did not always do the homework requested of them, and often participants did not always attend all sessions. With longer sessions, over a short period of time, to miss one session is to miss a substantial portion of the course. We would like to explore more seriously contractual arrangements with carers, in terms of both attendance and between-session work. Social workers in social services departments have also indicated a willingness to help in these regards.

3. Where there were two carers we were keen to involve both wherever possible. This meant that we allocated 12 foster carer units to each group, but in some cases we had groups that were larger because both partners came. This contributed to the 'crowding' of the programme and the 'squeeze' on space to cover all aspects in depth e.g. it took longer to 'turn-take' in discussions, and it was more difficult to involve everyone in practical examples. This was a major factor in moving from three-hour sessions to five-hour sessions between the first two groups and the remaining four. It helped, but did not solve these problems. Were we to run these groups, again we think they should be smaller, probably with a maximum of eight participants.

4. The training programme needs to be longer. There is simply too much to absorb, try out, check out and implement, to be optimally managed in a four-week programme. In a recently reported study by Pallett et al. (2002) a similar programme for foster carers ran over a ten-week period, for three-hour sessions. This is probably a minimum duration to achieve good results in complex circumstances, and three-hour sessions are probably easier for carers to attend (although the Pallett et al. study was conducted in inner city London, rather than the more rural areas we were working in).

5. We needed to focus much more explicitly and intensively on developing an understanding of cognitive-behavioural interventions, and expertise in their deployment. This has implications for the length of the programme that we have already discussed, and for the kind of teaching methods used. We had planned to use much more in the way of behaviour rehearsal of interventions as well as analysis (which we achieved) and we think the results testify to this deficit.

6.   It is also the case that in a handful of cases we were working with participants who had limited ability to grasp some core concepts. These problems have been noticed elsewhere (see Dutes 1985). This suggests that it might be worthwhile to screen participants for group programmes and/or to offer other carers a more individualised programme.

Broader contextual factors

Carers were often looking after extremely difficult children, in extremely difficult circumstances. Many of the children's scores on the Child Wellbeing Checklist fell within the 'clinical range (for Total Scores, and Sub-scales), and many more were in the borderline range. Often the carers were concerned about problems that were clearly 'clinical' in nature, e.g. Attention Deficit Hyperactivity Disorder; conduct disorders, and we were obliged to direct them to expert help. The problem with the latter was, frankly, that the carers had often been seeking such help for many years, and others who had secured it found it less than useful. It seemed at times that the most suitable candidates for training in learning theory and cognitive behavioural methods were the very clinicians to whom these children were being referred. For these children, behaviour management was necessary but not sufficient. It is not surprising that insofar as the behaviour problems that carers were facing were the manifestation of much more substantial difficulties, the study showed no differences in the rates of placement breakdown (see also below).

The carers had also to manage behaviour in quite extraordinary conditions. Sometimes, these were simply that departmental guidelines or procedures made it impossible for them to do what other parents might e.g. withhold pocket money, or bar a child's exit. Our considered view is that in some local authorities (because these guidelines did vary) there is a need to review guidelines in the light of what is in the child's best interest, as assessed in terms of living as 'normal' a life as possible. We encountered no foster carer who thought smacking was right, or who wanted to do anything that was remotely dubious, but they were often frustrated that their hands were tied with regard to doing what they thought was right. This was particularly so with regard to the child's long-term interests. For example, sometimes carers would take a stand with a particular child who would then ring his or her social worker and complain. This might lead to a move to another placement. The carers' complaints (essentially behavioural in nature) were that such action prevented a child from having to deal with a problem and/or from learning about the relationship between behaviour and consequences. It also prevented carers from influencing behaviour in a positive way i.e. providing consistency in a loving environment. More seriously, in their view, was that what many children learned was that they never had to face the consequences of their actions.

Difficult circumstances extended also to the lack of support that carers felt in relation to the child's social worker. We had strict rules within the groups about not 'whinging' - and we needed them. Foster carers often complained that it was impossible to get hold of a social worker (some had children to whom no worker had been allocated for over a year), that social workers often adopted an adversarial approach, and were more interested in the parents' rights that the child's welfare, and sometimes actively undermined their endeavours. These problems are not new, but it was clear that local authorities (and social workers) varied in the ways they were perceived from the very supportive to the downright 'couldn't care less'.

Practically, some foster carers were being asked to manage the unmanageable, like the single carer asked to cope with three very difficult children. Care continues to be needed in placement decisions, not only in terms of competing needs amongst looked-after children, but with regard to what carers can reasonably be asked to manage. To do otherwise inevitably impacts on the children anyway.

A good cognitive-behavioural principle is that people need opportunities to practice skills, to receive feedback and then to integrate that feedback into future 'performance'. It is difficult in any context to be given information and advice and be expected to implement it – often in its fine detail – in challenging circumstances. We think that carers who attend such training programmes need to have access to 'on hand' and ongoing advice from someone trained in cognitive-behavioural methods. Some carers suggested a monthly 'clinic' where they could come and discuss their concerns and their attempts to deal with difficulties. Others indicated they would like someone they could telephone for advice, and, indeed, at several points in the programme carers tried to secure such help from one or other of the trainers. From discussions with staff in some of the participating social services departments, there is support for such ideas. Family placement workers in particular are keen to support their carers, but often they lack the necessary expertise. One of the original features of this study was that if the training proved to be effective, we would explore ways of training social services staff to participate in training and to be able to offer ongoing support.

The first lesson from this project is that it is feasible to conduct randomised controlled trials of social interventions in social work and social care. This is something the funders are to be congratulated upon, not just in terms of their preparedness to commission such a study, but also to collaborate in ensuring its success. This collaboration extended to many in the various departments who also lent their support. The experience of doing this study has highlighted a number of important areas for consideration though. Most of these lessons are not new. Some might see them as evidence of the impracticality of experimental studies. We see them as areas for attention in future studies, irrespective of study design. Experimental methodology throws a spotlight on the problems inherent in all evaluative research.

Some of the points we wish to make are not just methodological. The nature of some of the difficulties we encountered indicates practice issues that also need to be considered. Some overlap with points already made above. In brief, these issues are as follows:

1.   It is not sufficient to have high level authorisation for research. This study ran into difficulties at various points because there was relatively little 'ownership' of the training programme or the evaluation. Individuals were, indeed, enthusiastic and supportive, but they did not always have the resources to follow-through promptly on agreements. It takes relatively little to delay a programme, and such delays occurred at the front end of this study for such reasons.

2.   Data Protection laws make it difficulty directly to access would-be participants in a study. If access could be facilitated early on in a project, then this would be helpful. Different authorities had different policies in this area. The delays at the outset seriously undermined our ability to allocate carers to age-banded groups (i.e. under 10s and over 10s). This did, we think, mean the first two groups were less successful than later ones (see earlier comments by Carer 07 above).

3.   At the outset we had hoped to strengthen the statistical power of the study by allocating one in four participants to the intervention group. We soon realised that this was unlikely to be possible, hence the inclusion of two other, large departments. Even then, we were barely able to recruit sufficient participants to randomise. This was partly attributable to the organisational problems referred to in (1) above, and also because it is quite difficult for carers to make arrangements to attend

training (even though we paid transport costs and child care fees). More importantly though, training does not appear to be a mainstream expectation amongst carers generally (as reported to us by those who attended the programme, and by family placement staff). Given the nature of the difficulties that carers are dealing with, training should surely be a requirement of continued registration? The limited sample from which foster carers were allocated, and the wide geographical area from which they were drawn, essentially meant that we had to make three separate allocations i.e. conduct three mini-trials. This will certainly have undermined the potential of the study to demonstrate effectiveness.

4. We took great care to explain the process of randomisation to all those who indicated a willingness to participate in the study, but nonetheless we 'lost' a number of people who were outraged that they were not in the 'training' group.

5. Rigorous evaluation is relatively costly, not least because one has to collect data from respondents who are not receiving the intervention being evaluated. Without these data, however, it is difficult to draw any conclusions about efficacy.

6. Even the best evaluation rarely provides a simple answer to questions of effectiveness, particularly in a field as complex as this. In an ideal world, one would have developed and piloted the training programme on several occasions, before mounting a 'full-blown' evaluation of the kind undertaken here. Such a developmental phase would certainly have highlighted the need for a longer programme, which focused more heavily on developing concrete skills in interventions strategies. The evaluation has now highlighted these, and a number of other issues and possibilities that it would be wise to follow through. This is one option. The other is to draw a line under the study, and file it. To do the latter would, in our view, represent a wasted investment, not only of public funds, but of the time given so generously by all those who participated. It would also deprive us of an opportunity to improve outcomes for children looked after.

7. We would like to suggest that there are sufficient data here (both relating to the achievements of the programme, and what is needed to enhance its effectiveness) to merit further development work and continued monitoring.

Chapter nine

Conclusions

Evidence of ineffectiveness is not the same as no evidence of effectiveness. The conclusions of this study certainly do not reflect the former. The results of this study suggest that it may have failed to secure evidence of the effectiveness of cognitive-behavioural methods due to problems in the execution of the study (three trials rather than one) and problems associated with a training programme. The resources invested in this study are such that it is worth investigating whether attending to some of these problems might improve the outcomes. In short, the indications are that the apparent lack of effectiveness in several areas might have been attributable, at least in part, to:

(i) organisational difficulties which impacted upon the strength of the study to address those aims

(ii) limitations in the length and effective content of the programme, and

(iii) a lack of available support to help foster carers implement newly-acquired skills.

In terms of their perceived need for such training, their overall satisfaction with the programme, and the evidence from Course Tasks, the programme was seen as a significant source of advice, knowledge and skills development. Many carers commented that the programme should be a requirement of all new foster carers.

We would, therefore, like to recommend that a revised programme be made available to the control group, and their progress monitored. The following changes would be desirable, based on the data from the current evaluation:

1. This programme should be longer in duration, and ensure that foster carers have opportunities to 'practice' intervention skills within the programme, and between sessions.

2.	Groups should be smaller, with a maximum of eight participants (whether couples or single carers).

3.	One of the difficulties we encountered during the programme was poor attendance on the part of some carers. We would like to recommend that a more contractual approach to attendance and homework be considered, although we appreciate that the present 'gift relationship' between carers and departments makes this difficult. It might be possible to consider an incentive to carers, such as a one-off cash payment to carers who complete the programme in full. This is a relatively modest price to pay, compared with mounting an expensive programme which participants do not use to the full.

4.	Family placement social workers (or their equivalent) should be invited to participate in the groups, and should be offered (separately) a three-day programme to develop their knowledge and skills in cognitive-behavioural work. They should then be a point of contact for foster carers seeking advice.

5.	Alternatively, or perhaps as well, a monthly 'problem clinic' could be considered within each local authority for carers who have participated in training. This should be run by someone with competence in cognitive-behavioural skills and child development.

ENDNOTES While there is general agreement among researchers concerning an acceptable level of type I error – namely, a = .05 – there is no such consensus concerning an acceptable level of type II error or power. In the absence of such agreement, the recommendation of Jacob Cohen (1965, pp. 98-99; 1988, pp. 53-56) and others (e.g., Hinkle & Oliver, 1983; Keppel, 1991, p.75; and Kirk, 1982, p. 144) was followed in that power be set at .80 for most research in the behavioural sciences. This translates in that the study is expected to produce significant results 80 percent of the time and non-significant results 20 percent of the time.   In this study we decided to describe the estimated treatment effects as "medium" (cf. Cohen, 1988) – that is, we anticipated that the experiment will produce an estimated omega squared of at least $\omega^2_A = .06$. The following formula was used for the calculation:

$$\eta' = \phi^2 \left(\frac{1 - \omega^2_A}{\omega^2_A} \right)$$

where η' is the estimated sample size we wish to determine, the quantity ϕ (phi) is a statistic that we obtain from the table reported by Rotton and Schönemann (1978) and ω^2_A is the estimate of the size of the treatment effect. In this particular study, for degree of power .80 with a=2 treatment condition, i.e., df=1, the estimate of ϕ is 2. By substituting these values in the above equation we get η' = 62.67. This means we need at least 63 subjects per condition to achieve power .80 when the anticipated results are of "medium" size. Due to low response rate, attrition during the course of the study, time and financial restrictions, considerations about the appropriate sample size as shown by the results of the power analysis could not be adhered to.

References

Aldgate, J. and Hawley, D. (1986) *Recollections of Disruption: a study of foster home breakdowns.* London: National Foster Care Association.

Altman, D.G. (1997) *Practical statistics for medical research.* London: Chapman & Hall.

Bandura, A. (1982) 'Self-efficacy mechanism in human agency'. *American Psychologist*, **37**, 122-147.

Barlow, J. (1997) *Systematic review of the effectiveness of parent-training programmes in improving behaviour problems in children aged 3-10 years.* Oxford: Health Services Research Unit, Department of Public Health, University of Oxford.

Barlow, J. (1999) *Systematic review of the effectiveness of parent-training programmes in improving behaviour problems in children aged 3-10 years* (2nd ed.). Oxford: Health Services Research Unit, Department of Public Health, University of Oxford.

Bennett, D.S. and Gibbons, T.A. (2000) 'Efficacy of child cognitive-behavioural interventions for antisocial behavior: A meta-analysis'. *Child and Family behaviour Therapy, 22,* 1-15.

Berridge, D. and Cleaver, H. (1987) *Foster Home Breakdown.* Oxford: Basil Blackwell.

Berry, M.A. (1988) 'A review of parent training programs in child welfare.' *Social Service Review*, **62**, 303-323.

Borland, M., O'Hara, G. and Triseliotis, J. (1991) 'Placement outcomes for children with special needs.' *Adoption and Fostering,* **15**, 2, 18-28.

Boyd, L.H., Jr. and Remy, L.L. (1978) 'Is foster parent training worthwhile?' *Social Service Review, 52,* 275-295.

Brestan, E. V. & Eyeberg, S. M. (1998) 'Effective psychosocial treatments of conduct-disordered children and adolescents: 29 years, 82 studies, 5,272 kids.' *Journal of Clinical Child Psychology*, **27**, 180-189.

Brown, D.L. (1980) *A comparative study of the effects of two foster parent training methods on attitudes of parental acceptance, sensitivity to children, and general foster parent attitudes.* Doctoral Dissertation, Michigan State University.

Burry, C.L. (1995) *Evaluation of a training program for prospective foster parents to increase their specialized competencies and intent to foster infants with prenatal substance effects.* UMI Dissertation Services.

Burry, C.L. (1999) 'Evaluation of a training program for foster parents of infants with prenatal substance effects.' *Child Welfare*, **78**, 197-214.

Campbell, D.T. and Stanley, J.C. (1973) *Experimental and Quasi-Experimental Designs for Research.* Chicago: Rand McNally College Publishing Company.

Cedar, B. and Levant, R.F. (1990) 'A meta-analysis of the effects of parent effectiveness training.' *American Journal of Family Therapy,* **18**, 373-384.

Chamberlain, P., Moreland, S. and Reid, K. (1992) 'Enhanced service and stipends for foster parents: Effects on retention rates and outcomes for children.' *Child Welfare*, **71**, 387-401.

Chamberlain, P., Moreland, S., & Reid, K. (1992) 'Enhanced service and stipends for foster parents: Effects on retention rates and outcomes for children'. *Child Welfare*, **71**, 387-401.

Cobb, E.J., Leitenberg, H., & Burchard, J.D. (1982) 'Foster parents teaching foster parents: Communication and conflict resolution skills training.' *Journal of Community Psychology,* **10**, 240-249.

Department of Health (1991) *Patterns and Outcomes in Child Placement,* London: HMSO.

Department of Health (2001) *Social services performance assessment framework indicators, 2000-2001.* London: National Statistics.

Department of Health (2002) *The Children Act Report 2001.* London: Department of Health.

Dimigen, G., Del Priore, C., Butler, S., Ferguson, L and Swan, M. (1996) 'Psychiatric disorder among children at time of entering local authority care: questionnaire survey.' *British Medical Journal,* **319**, 675.

Dutes, J.C. (1985) *A comparative investigation of the effectiveness of two foster parent training programs.* Unpublished Doctoral Dissertation, Michigan State University.

George, V. (1970) *Foster Care – Theory and Practice.* London: Routledge, Kegan and Paul.

Guerney, L.F. (1977) 'A description and evaluation of a skills training program for foster parents.' *American Journal of Community Psychology*, **5**, 361-371.

Hampson, R. (1985) 'Foster parent training: Assessing its role in upgrading foster home care.' In M. Cox & R. Cox (Eds.), *Foster care: Current issues, policies, and practices* (167-201). Greenwich, CT: Ablex Publishing Corp.

Hampson, R.B., & Tavormina, J.B. (1980) 'Relative effectiveness of behavioral and reflective group training with foster mothers.' *Journal of Consulting & Clinical Psychology*, **48**, 294-295.

Hampson, R.B., Shulte, M.A., & Ricks, C.C. (1983) 'Individual vs. group training for foster parents: Efficiency/effectiveness evaluations.' *Family Relations*, **32**, 191-201.

Herbert, M. and Wookey, J. (In press) Managing Disruptive Behaviour: The Child-Wise Parenting Skills Approach. Chichester: John Wiley.

Hill-Tout, I., Lowe, K., Pithouse, A. and Shepstone, K. (2001) 'Managing Challenging Behaviour in Foster Care: Identifying Best Practice Through Training and Evaluation.' www.word.dial.pipex.com

Katz, S.J. (1977) *Psycho-social effects of parent training on the quality of the foster parent-child relationship.* Doctoral Dissertation, University of California, Los Angeles, 1977.. *Dissertation Abstracts International*, **38**, 2558A – 2559A.

Keane, A. (1983) 'Behaviour Problems Among Long-term Foster Children.' *Adoption and Fostering, 7*, 3, 53-62.

Lee, J.H. and Holland, T.P. (1991) 'Evaluating the effectiveness of foster parent training.' *Research on Social Work Practice,* **1**, 162-174.

Levant, R.F., & Geer, M.F. (1981) 'A systematic skills approach to the selection and training of foster parents as mental health paraprofessionals, I: Project overview and selection component.' *Journal of Community Psychology,* **9**, 224-230.

Levant, R.F., Slattery, S.C. and Slobodian, P.E. (1981) 'A systematic skills approach to the selection and training of foster parents as mental health paraprofessionals, II: Training.' *Journal of Community Psychology*, **9**, 224-230.

McCann, J.B., James, A., Wilson, S. and Dunn, G. (1996) 'Prevalence of psychiatric disorders in young people in the care system.' *British Medical Journal*, **313**, 1529.

Meichenbaum, D.H. (1977). *Cognitive-behavior modification: an integrative approach.* New York: Plenum Press.

Meichenbaum, D.H. & Turk, D. (1982) 'Stress, coping and disease: a cognitive behavioral perspective. In R.W.J. Newfeld (Ed.), *Psychological stress and psychopathology.* New York: Hill Book Company.

Milham, S., Bullock, R., Hosie, K. and Haak, M. (1986) *Lost in Care: the Problems of Maintaining Links between Children in Care and their Families.* Aldershot: Gower.

Napier, H. (1972) 'Success and Failure in Foster Care.' *British Journal of Social Work*, **2**, 2, 187-204.

Nissim, R. and Simm, M. (1994) 'Linking Research Evidence and Practice in Fostering Work – the Art of the Possible.' *Adoption and Fostering,* **18**, 4, 10-17.

O'Dell, S.L., Tarler-Belolo, L. and Flynn, J.M. (1979) 'An instrument to measure knowledge of behavioural principles as applied to children.' *Journal of Behavioral Therapy & Experimental Psychiatry*, **10**, 29-34.

Packman, J., Randall, J. and Jacques, N. (1986) *Who Needs Care? Social Work Decisions About Children.* Oxford: Basil Blackwell.

Pallett, C., Scott, S., Blackeby, K., Yule, W. and Weissman, R. (2002) 'Fostering change: a cognitive-behavioural approach to help foster carers manage children.' *Adoption and Fostering,* April.

Parker, R. (1966) *Decisions in Child Care. A Study of Prediction in Fostering.* London: Allen and Unwin.

Penn, J.V. (1978) 'A model for training foster parents in behavior modification techniques.' *Child Welfare*, **57**, 175-180.

Quinton, D., Rushton, A., Dance, C. and Mayes, D. (1998) *Joining New Families: A study of adoption and fostering in middle childhood.* Chichester: John Wiley and Sons.

Romero, B. (1995) *A study of the behavioural and emotional problems of children fostered by Surrey County Council: the foster carers' perspectives.* MSc Dissertation, Royal Holloway, University of London.

Rowe, J. and Lambert, L. (1973) *Children Who Wait: a study of children needing substitute families.* London: Association of British Adoption and Fostering Agencies.

Rowe, J., Cain, H., Hundleby, M. and Keane, A. (1984) *Long Term Fostering.* London: Batsford/BAAF.

Serketich, W.J. and Dumas, J.E. (1996) 'The effectiveness of behavioural parent training to modify anti-social behaviour in children: a meta-analysis.' *Behavior Therapy*, **27**, 171-186.

Simon, R.D. and Simon, D.K. (1982) ' The effects of foster parent selection and training on service delivery.' *Children and Youth Services Review*, **3**, 515-524.

Thoburn, J. and Rowe, L. (1991) In Fratter, J., Rowe, J., Sapsford, D. and Thoburn, J. (Eds) *Permanent Family Placement: a Decade of Experience.* London: BAAF.

Thomas, N. and Beckett, C. (1994) 'Are Children Still Waiting? Recent developments and the impact of the Children Act 1989. *Adoption and Fostering,* **18**, 1, 8-16.

Thorpe, R. (1980) 'The Experiences of Children and Parents Living Apart: implications and guidelines for practice' In Triseliotis, J. (Ed) *New Developments in Foster Care and Adoption.* London: Routledge, Kegan Paul.

Todres, R. and Bunston, T. (1993) 'Parent education program evaluation: A review of the literature.' *Canadian Journal of Community Mental Health*, **12**, 225-257.

Triseliotis, J. (1987) 'Social workers and foster care.' in *In Whose Trust?* London: National Foster Care Association.

van de Wiel, N. Matthys, W., Cohen-Kettenis, P. C. and van Engeland, H. (2002) 'Effective treatments of school-aged conduct disordered children: recommendations for changing clinical and research practices.' *European Child & Adolescent Psychiatry.* **11** 2, 79-84.

Warren, D. (1997) *Foster Care in Crisis.* London: Foster Care Association.

Webster-Stratton, C. (1998) 'Parent-training with low-income families: promoting parental engagement through a collaborative approach.' In J.R. Lutzker (Ed) *Handbook of Child Abuse Research and Treatment.* New York: Plenum Press.

Webster-Stratton, C. and Herbert, M. (1994) *Troubled Families. Problem Children.* Chichester: John Wiley.

Weisz, J.R. (1997) 'Effects of interventions for child and adolescent psychological dysfunction: relevance of context, developmental factors, and individual differences.' In S.S. Luthar, J.A. Burack, D. Cicchetti & J.R. Weisz (Eds), *Developmental Psychopathology: Perspectives on adjustment, risk, and disorder.* New York: Cambridge University Press.

Woolfenden S. R., Williams K., Peat J. (2003) 'Family and parenting interventions in children and adolescents with conduct disorder and delinquency aged 10-17 (Cochrane Review).' In: The Cochrane Library, Issue 1, 2003. Oxford: Update Software.

Zukoski, M. (1999) 'Foster parent training.' In J.A. Silver, B.J. Amster, & T. Haecker (1999). *Young children and foster care. A guide for professionals.* London: Paul H. Brookes Publishing.

Appendicies

Appendix 1 **The Knowledge of Behavioral Principles As Applied to Children (KBPAC)**

The *Knowledge of Behavioural principles As Applied to Children* (KBPAC) is a 50-item multiple forced-choice test designed to assess understanding of the application of basic behavioural principles with children.

Administration requires 30-60 minutes.

The questions avoid behavioural vocabulary and most present practical problem situations to which the respondent is to select the response that has the greatest probability of producing the desired effect. Other issues covered include basic behavioural assumptions about behaviour change, principles in the use of reinforcement and punishment, schedules, shaping, counting and recording, differential attention and extinction.

The criterion response for each question was selected on the basis of learning principles. The Kuder-Richardson reliability coefficient is .94, and the odd-even split-half correlation is .93. The instrument has been found useful for research and educational assessment purposes where such a general measure of verbal knowledge of behavioural principles is needed.

Appendix 2 Course Task

Between now and the follow-up day, we would like you to design an intervention to tackle at least *ONE* aspect of behaviour that is problematic for a young person you are caring for, or may care.

This pack takes you through the key steps in assessment, goal setting, monitoring and evaluation. It also contains a brief summary of the kinds of behavioural strategies that can be useful, and the kinds of situations that it might be appropriate to use them in. The Handbook accompanying the course contains more information about each of these stages.

Please contact *Geraldine Macdonald* if you have any queries or problems. Geraldine can be contacted on either 0117 954 6718 (day-time) or 0117 946 6603 (evenings and weekends).

Name of course participant...

The young person concerned is: male ❑ **female** ❑ (*please tick as appropriate*)

The young person concerned is aged _____ years. (*Please state age in years*)

What to do

During the course we looked at the basic approaches to assessing a problem and choosing strategies and tactics for handling them. We want you to try to use these to tackle at least one aspect of difficult or challenging behaviour in one of the children or young people for whom you care. We appreciate that this can be difficult.

We know that you have a great deal to do, and we appreciate that your job is 'round the clock'. However, we hope that by improving your knowledge of problem behaviour, its causes, the ways in which it can be maintained, and some of the ways to tackle it, that you will feel less pressured and/or more confident in your abilities as professional carers. The snag is that the only way to achieve this is by practising – and learning by trial and error.

The follow-up day

The follow-up day will be based on people's experiences of using cognitive-behavioural approaches. It will look at what worked, what didn't work. It will explore the problems you encountered and whether or not there are ways of solving these. We will discuss the timing of the follow-up day at the end of this session.

How to proceed

The next page is a summary of the stages of problem-solving that we have looked at during the course. We would like you to use this as a guide. We also provide a summary sheet of the range of interventions with some guidance as to what interventions are appropriate for what kinds of problems and/ or behaviour. Children and young people are highly individual. Whilst are few general rules that can be applied 'across the board', which is why assessment (being specific, tracking occurrences of behaviour and looking at its antecedents and consequences) is so important. Helping children and young people overcome problematic ways of behaving is not easy. Sometimes there are 'quick fixes' but more often than not it is more challenging. The only way to develop our expertise is to practice. This is what we are asking you to do. We are not looking for 'success stories' (although these would be welcome!) but we want to understand how best to help people doing one of the most difficult jobs there is. Please help us to do this, if you can.

The behaviour I am concerned about is:

Please describe in the space below. Please be specific. Don't use terms such as 'temper tantrum' or 'rude' or 'violent'. State clearly what the young person says or does in sufficient detail that someone would recognise it (and therefore be able to *count* it).

The most common 'triggers' for the behaviour are:

Please use the 'ABC' method for helping to identify the sorts of things or situations (people, places, times) that seem to trigger the behaviour you have described above.

The 'pay-off' for the behaviour appears to be:

Using the 'ABC' method, state briefly what sorts of things most often follow the behaviour that you would like to change? What do you think is the 'pay-off' for the young person?

How serious is the problem?

Some problems are very serious but are not necessarily very frequent. If the behaviour you want to influence happens on a daily basis, please record the occurrences on the *Intervention Chart* (page 5). If it does not occur so frequently, use the *frequency chart* (page 4) and note when your intervention begins by drawing a line from top to bottom

What is your goal?

Please state clearly what you would like your child/young person to be doing (more often) and/or doing less often (or not at all).

What interventions did you choose?

How successful was the intervention?

Please tick one:

Very successful - the behaviour improved ❏

Not at all successful - the behaviour did not change ❏

Quite successful - there was some improvement in the behaviour ❏

The behaviour got worse ❏

Please elaborate if you can

What were the main problems you encountered?

Frequency Chart

NAME:

Use the chart to record any instance of behaviour on a daily basis.

Behaviour:

	1	2	3	4	5	6	7	8	9	10	11	12	13	14	15	16	17	18	19	20		
20																						
19																						
18																						
17																						
16																						
15																						
14																						
13																						
12																						
11																						
10																						
9																						
8																						
7																						
6																						
5																						
4																						
3																						
2																						
1																						

Days

Specify the behaviour being monitored:

Collecting Data:

One Week Baseline, Intervention and Follow Up

NAME:

Use the chart to record any instance of behaviour. The chart is divided into a 'baseline period' of 7 days (marked by the thick black line) and an 'intervention period'. Recording the behaviour throughout the intervention period will give a picture of how effective the intervention is proving to be.

Behaviour:

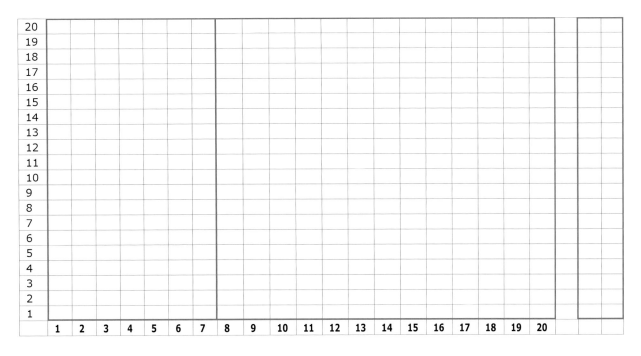

Days

Baseline   *Intervention*   *Follow-up*

ABC RECORD SHEET

ANTECEDENTS (what leads up to the event)	BEHAVIOUR (the actual event)	CONSEQUENCES (what happened afterwards)	I felt……

Tactics

This is a 'bare bones' summary of some key tactics. Please refer to the Handbook for other ideas and for more information in each.

Tactics to *increase* wanted behaviour

1. **Positive reinforcement**
   - Social reinforcers, e.g. praise, encouragement. These are the reinforcers that keep behaviour going once the next two have done their work. They need to be given 'hand in hand' with them.
   - Tangible rewards, e.g. sweets, treats, outings. Important for young children in particular
   - Generalisable or symbolic reinforcers, e.g. stars, tokens, points. Things that can be exchanged for other things at predetermined times.

2. **Premack's principle or 'Grandma's rule'** i.e. when you do this, then you can do that. What is required first is something that the young person is less inclined to do. What they want to do most depends on doing this first, e.g. when you do the dishes, then you can go out to play/with your friends.

3. **Differential reinforcement.** This is really a combined tactic which increases one behaviour whilst at the same time trying to decrease another. The general idea is that one reinforces a behaviour that is incompatible with the behaviour one want to see less of, e.g. reinforcing sharing and co-operation as a tactic for decreasing fighting and arguing. The latter would be ignored as far as possible, or perhaps 'punished'.

Tactics to decrease unwanted behaviour

1. **Judicious or planned ignoring.** Must be done neutrally and consistently. Not appropriate when the behaviour is dangerous to the young person or to others.

2. **Logical consequences.** Trying to ensure that if a child does something such as stealing or damaging property or hurting other people, that s/he is required to do something that is logically related to that e.g., repairing the damage or tidying up, saying sorry and trying to make amends.

3. **Time out.** The proper name is Time Out from Positive Reinforcement. It entails removing a child from all positive forms of reinforcement (especially attention). Not suitable for older children, but it is also possible for carers to 'remove themselves'. See the Carer's Handbook for more information.

4. **Response cost.** 'Fining' a child (by removing opportunities, money - for those circumstances where this is possible - or other pleasant activities) in a pre-determined way. Usually combined with reinforcement for keeping to agreements in a contract etc.

5. **Contract and negotiation.** Suitable for young people where there is conflict and where compromises need to be reached, for a variety of reasons. Teaching communication skills, problem-solving skills and communication training can all be part of this process. Role-reversal (asking young person to take the role of carer and encourage them to think through what that would feel like, what the worries might be, etc. and vice versa) has been shown to be an effective way of enhancing negotiated settlements. Taking it in turns to say one's piece, without interruption, and making sure that everyone's opinion is heard and understood are also important components of these approaches.